276 EDIBLE
WILD PLANTS

OF THE

UNITED STATES & CANADA

Berries, Roots, Nuts, Greens, Flowers, and Seeds

CALEB WARNOCK

Published by Familius LLC, www.familius.com

PO Box 1249 Reedley 93654

Familius books are available at special discounts for bulk purchases, whether for
sales promotions or for family or corporate use. For more information, email
orders@familius.com. Reproduction of this book in any manner, in whole or in
part, without written permission of the publisher is prohibited.

Inherent dangers exist when ingesting wild plants. The material in this book
is presented for general information purposes only. The publisher and author
accept no liability of any kind. Any application of the information in this book
is at the sole discretion and responsibility of the user.

Special thanks to the Washington Department of Ecology
for the use of their image of Typha glauca.

Library of Congress Control Number: 2019953190

Print ISBN 9781641702423

Ebook ISBN 9781641702829

Printed in China

Edited by Peg Sandkam and Kaylee Mason

Cover design by Carlos Guerrero

Book design by Emma Hiatt

10 9 8 7 6 5 4 3 2 1

First Edition

CALEB WARNOCK

276 EDIBLE
WILD PLANTS

OF THE

UNITED STATES & CANADA

Berries, Roots, Nuts, Greens, Flowers, and Seeds

FAMILIUS

CONTENTS

Welcome to the World of Wild Foods 1

PART ONE: THE PLANTS

1 *Abutilon theophrasti* (velvetleaf)

2 *Acer negundo* (box elder maple)

3 *Achillea millefolium* (Western yarrow)

4 *Aegilops cylindrica* (jointed goatgrass)

5 *Agastache foeniculum* (blue giant hyssop)

6 Amaranthus Species

7 *Amaranthus albus* (tumble pigweed)

8 *Amaranthus blitoides* (mat amaranth, prostrate pigweed)

9 *Amaranthus hybridus* (slim amaranth)

10 *Amaranthus powellii* (Powell's amaranth)

11 *Amaranthus retroflexus* (redroot pigweed, redroot amaranth)

12 *Amaranthus tuberculatus* (roughfruit amaranth)

13 *Amelanchier alnifolia* (Saskatoon serviceberry)

14 *Arctium minus* (lesser burdock)

15 *Argentina anserina* (silverweed cinquefoil)

16 *Artemisia frigida* (fringed sagebrush)

17 Asclepias Species

18 *Asclepias incarnata* (swamp milkweed)

19 *Asclepias syriaca* (common milkweed)

20 *Asclepias verticillata* (whorled milkweed)

21 *Asclepias viridiflora* (green comet milkweed)

22 Avena Species

23 *Avena fatua* (wild oat)

24 *Avena sativa* (common oat)

25 Barbarea Species

26 *Barbarea vulgaris* (garden yellowrocket)

27 *Barbarea orthoceras* (American yellowrocket)

28 Brassica Species

29 *Brassica juncea* (brown mustard)

30 *Brassica napus* (grape mustard)

31 *Brassica nigra* (black mustard)

32 *Brassica rapa* (field mustard)

33 Bromus Species

34 *Bromus japonicus* (Japanese brome, field brome)

35 *Bromus secalinus* (cheat, rye brome)

36 *Bromus tectorum* (downy brome, cheat grass)

37 *Calypso bulbosa* (fairy slipper)

38 *Calystegia sepium* (hedge bindweed)

39 Camelina Species

40 *Camelina microcarpa* (lesser gold of pleasure)

41 *Camelina sativa* (gold of pleasure)

42 *Campanula rapunculoides* (creeping bellflower)

43 *Capsella bursa-pastoris* (shepherd's purse)

44 *Cardamine pensylvanica* (Pennsylvania bittercress)

45 *Cardaria draba* (whitetop, hoary cress)

46 *Carduus nutans* (musk thistle)

47 *Carum carvi* (common caraway)

48 *Celtis occidentalis* (hackberries)

49 *Cenchrus longispinus* (longspine sandbur)

50 *Centaurea cyanus* (garden cornflower)

51 Chamerion Species

52 *Chamerion angustifolium* (fireweed)

53 *Chamerion latifolium* (dwarf fireweed)

54 Chenopodium Species

55 *Chenopodium album* (lamb's-quarters, wild spinach)

56 *Chenopodium berlandieri* (goosefoot, netseed lamb's-quarters)

57 *Chenopodium murale* (nettleleaf goosefoot)

58 *Chorispora tenella* (blue mustard)

59 *Cichorium intybus* (chicory)

60 Cirsium Species

61 *Cirsium arvense* (Canada thistle)

62 *Cirsium vulgare* (common thistle, bull thistle)

63 *Cleome serrulata* (Rocky Mountain bee plant)

64 *Convolvulus arvensis* (field bindweed)

65 *Conyza canadensis* (horseweed)

66 Cornus Species

67 *Cornus canadensis* (creeping dogwood)

68 *Cornus sericea* (Western dogwood)

69 *Corylus cornuta* (beaked hazelnut)

70 Crataegus Species

71 *Crataegus chrysocarpa* (red haw tree)

72 *Crataegus succulenta* (fleshy hawthorn)

73 Crepis Species

74 *Crepis capillaris* (smooth hawksbeard)

75 *Crepis nana* (dwarf alpine hawksbeard)

76 *Cycloloma atriplicifolium* (winged pigweed)

77 *Cynoglossum officinale* (houndstongue, gypsyflower)

78 Cypernus Species

79 *Cyperus erythrorhizos* (redroot flatsedge)

80 *Cyperus esculentus* (yellow nutsedge)

81 *Cyperus odoratus* (fragrant flatsedge)

82 *Cyperus schweinitzii* (Schweinitz's flatsedge)

83 *Cyperus squarrosus* (bearded flatsedge)

84 *Daucus carota* (wild carrot)

85 Descurainia Species

86 *Descurainia pinnata* (Western tansy mustard)

87 *Descurainia sophia* (flixweed, herb sophia)

88 *Digitaria sanguinalis* (hairy crabgrass)

89 Elaeagnus Species

90 *Elaeagnus angustifolia* (Russian olive)

91 *Elaeagnus commutata* (silverberry)

92 *Eleusine indica* (goosegrass)

93 *Elymus repens* (harsh Indian paintbrush)

94 Equisetum Species

95 *Equisetum arvense* (horsetail grass)

96 *Equisetum laevigatum* (smooth horsetail)

97 *Equisetum hyemale* (scouringrush horsetail)

98 *Equisetum pratense* (meadow horsetail)

99 *Equisetum scirpoides* (dwarf scouringrush)

100 *Equisetum variegatum* (variegated scouringrush)

101 *Erodium cicutarium* (redstem filaree, stork's bill)

102 Fragaria Species

103 *Fragaria vesca* (woodland, alpine, or wild strawberry)

104 *Fragaria virginiana* (Virginia strawberry)

105 *Galium aparine* (cleavers, goosegrass)

106 *Gaultheria hispidula* (creeping snowberry)

107 *Geranium bicknellii* (Bicknell's cranesbill)

108 Helianthus Species

109 *Helianthus annuus* (common sunflower)

110 *Helianthus maximiliani* (Maximilian sunflower)

111 *Helianthus pauciflorus* (stiff sunflower)

112 *Helianthus petiolaris* (prairie sunflower)

113 *Helianthus tuberosus* (sunchokes, Jerusalem artichoke)

114 *Hibiscus trionum* (Venice mallow)

115 *Hordeum jubatum* (foxtail barley, squirrel-tail grass)

116 *Juglans nigra* (black walnut)

117 *Kochia scoparia* (kochia)

118 *Lactuca pulchella* (blue lettuce)

119 Lamium Species

120 *Lamium amplexicaule* (henbit)

121 *Lamium purpureum* (purple dead nettle)

122 *Lathyrus latifolius* (everlasting peavine, wild sweet pea)

123 *Lepidium perfoliatum* (clasping pepperweed)

124 *Lolium perenne* (Italian ryegrass)

125 *Lycium barbarum* (gojiberry, wolfberry)

126 *Lythrum salicaria* (purple loosestrife, purple lythrum)

127 *Malus domestica* (common apple)

128 *Malva neglecta* (common mallow)

129 *Matricaria discoidea* (pineapple weed)

130 Burclover Species

131 *Medicago lupulina* (black medic)

132 *Medicago polymorpha* (snooth hawksbeard)

133 *Medicago sativa* (alfalfa)

134 Sweetclover Species

135 *Melilotus albus* (white sweetclover)

136 *Melilotus indicas* (Indian sweetclover)

137 *Melilotus officinalis* (yellow sweetclover)

138 *Morus alba* (white mulberry)

139 *Nasturtium officinale* (watercress)

140 Opuntia Species

141 *Opuntia humifusa* (devil's tongue)

142 *Opuntia* (prickly pear)

143 Oxalis Species

144 *Oxalis corniculata* (creeping woodsorrel)

145 *Oxalis stricta* (yellow woodsorrel)

146 Panicum Species

147 *Panicum dichotomiflorum* (fall panicum)

148 *Panicum miliaceum* (wild-proso millet)

149 *Phragmites australis* (common reed)

150 Physalis Species

151 *Physalis heterophylla* (clammy groundcherry)

152 *Physalis longifolia* (longleaf groundcherry)

153 Plantain Species

154 *Plantago lanceolata* (narrowleaf plantain)

155 *Plantago major* (broadleaf plantain)

156 Polygonum Species

157 *Polygonum amphibium* (willow grass, water knotweed)

158 *Polygonum arenastrum* (small-leafed knotweed, oval-leaf knotweed)

159 *Polygonum cuspidatum* (Japanese knotweed)

160 *Polygonum lapathifolium* (curlytop knotweed)

161 *Polypogon monspeliensis* (rabbitfoot polypogon)

162 *Polygonum persicaria* (spotted ladysthumb)

163 *Portulaca oleracea* (common purslane)

164 Prunus Species

165 *Prunus americana* (American wild plum)

166 *Prunus pumila* (sandcherry)

167 *Prunus persica* (peach)

168 *Prunus serotina* (black cherry)

169 *Prunus virginiana* (Western chokecherry, black chokecherry)

170 Additional Prunus Species

171 *Pyrus communis* (common pear)

172 Raphanus Species

173 *Raphanus raphanistrum* (wild radish)

174 *Raphanus sativus* (garden radish)

175 *Rhus glabra* (smooth sumac)

176 Ribes Species

177 *Ribes aureum* (golden currant)

178 *Ribes americanum* (American black currant)

179 *Ribes lacustre* (prickly black currant)

180 Additional Ribes Species

181 Rose Species

182 *Rosa rubiginosa* (sweetbriar rose)

183 *Rosa woodsii* (Western wild rose)

184 Rubus Species

185 *Rubus flagellaris* (Northern dewberry)

186 *Rubus allegheniensis* (allegheny blackberry)

187 *Rubus armeniacus* (Himalayan blackberry)

188 *Rubus idaeus* (wild raspberries)

189 *Rubus occidentalis* (black raspberries)

190 Additional Rubus Species

191 Rumex Species

192 *Rumex acetosella* (sheep sorrel)

193 *Rumex crispus* (curly dock, yellow dock)

194 *Rumex obtusifolius* (broadleaf dock)

195 *Sagittaria cuneata* (wapato, arumleaf, arrowhead)

196 *Salsola tragus* (Russian thistle)

197 Sambucus Species

198 *Sambucus nigra* (blue elderberry)

199 *Sambucus racemosa* (red elderberry)

200 *Secale cereale* (cereal rye)

201 *Setaria pumila* (yellow foxtail)

202 Sowthistle Species

203 *Sonchus arvensis* (sowthistle)

204 *Sonchus asper* (spiny sowthistle)

205 *Sonchus oleraceus* (common sowthistle)

206 *Sorbus scopulina* (European mountain ash)

207 Sorghum Species

208 *Sorghum bicolor* (wild grain sorghum)

209 *Sorghum halepense* (johnsongrass)

210 *Stellaria media* (chickweed)

211 *Taraxacum officinale* (common dandelion)

212 *Thlaspi arvense* (field pennycress)

213 Tragopogon Species

214 *Tragopogon dubius* (yellow salsify)

215 *Tragopogon pratensis* (goat's beard, meadow salsify)

216 *Tragopogon porrifolius* (salsify)

217 Trifolium Species

218 *Trifolium hybridum* (alsike clover)

219 *Trifolium incarnatum* (crimson clover)

220 *Trifolium repens* (white clover, Dutch clover)

221 *Trifolium pratense* (red clover)

222 Additional Trifolium Species

223 Typha Species

224 *Typha angustifolia* (narrowleaf cattail)

225 *Typha glauca* (hybrid cattail)

226 *Typha latifolia* (broadleaf cattail)

227 *Urtica dioica* (stinging nettle)

228 Vaccinium Species (blueberries)

229 Addtional Vaccinium Species

230 *Viola canadensis* (Canadian white violet)

231 Vitus Species

232 *Vitis aestivalis* (summer grape)

233 *Vitis riparia* (riverbank rape)

234 Addtional Vitis Species

PART TWO: USEFUL LISTS, AND Q&A

235 Important for Food Value

236 Wild Edibles I Eat Most

237 Fruits & Berries

238 Significant Grains & Seeds

239 Nuts

240 Significant Roots & Tubers

241 Trees / Shrubs / Bushes

242 Poisons

243 Questions and Answers

As I write this introduction, I am at Cecret Lake, a crystal-clear alpine pool at 10,000-foot elevation in the Rocky Mountains. The icy water is populated with slow-moving tiger salamanders and surrounded by hundreds of species of wild flowers and wild edibles. The hike here is like walking down one long aisle in Mother Nature's grocery store—berries, grains, seeds, flowers. It takes me awhile to arrive at the lake because I taste my way up the trail. Several species of honeysuckle berries burst with juice in my mouth. The thimbleberries are delicate and better than any berry in any store. Seeing me picking and eating, an older couple stops to ask me if I know where the wild raspberries are. They haven't noticed they are standing less than ten feet away from two species of serviceberries, which are among my favorite berries of all time.

In about ten days, it will be time to make serviceberry jam once again because the mountains will be teeming with trees loaded with millions of sweet purple candy drops. The elderberries are just ripening. I will be making elderberry jam, syrup, and tinctures from the berries and leaves, as well as freezing whole fresh berries and drying other batches of berries for winter use. There are plenty of ripe edible wildflowers to taste—fireweed, mountain geranium, several species of onions. Salad greens are everywhere—nettle, dandelions, cress, fireweed leaves. Even the cattails lower in the canyon have not become fibrous yet. The gooseberries have their stripes but they are still green, a couple of weeks away from harvesting. There are a few last cleavers of the season in the shade of the aspens.

I eat wild edibles almost every day of the year, wherever I go—locally, across the country, and across the globe. I have eaten wild purslane in Portugal, happy to see its cheerful yellow flowers. I have eaten wild German chamomile at the German border. I eat extensively out of my backyard and my farm fields, in the deep desert, and in the yards of students, clients, and friends.

To make sure I have a supply of clean, organic wild foods available when I want them, I grow wild edibles in my garden spring, summer, and fall, and in my geothermal greenhouses in winter—and not just for eating, because as you will see in these pages, they have other valuable uses too. I have tackled a full discussion of how and when and what herbs to use as natural medicine in another book, but I do highlight on these pages some of the most important and popular medicinal herbs, berries, and roots that I use regularly.

Globally, roughly 10 percent of all plants are considered edible. Archeology and written history have proven repeatedly that most if not all of this 10 percent was widely eaten at some point. Since the advent of industrialization, the number of species we eat has fallen dramatically. Knowledge of what is edible—knowledge our ancestors three generations ago held deeply—has slipped away with astonishing speed.

Most books on wild edibles focus on greens. I wanted this book to be in the running for the most comprehensive book on wild edibles ever printed—a book that could be used for generations. Salad greens are great, but roots and grains and seeds and nuts are sustenance.

As a permaculture expert, I do property consultations, visiting people's homes to help them design the best gardens and landscapes for their specific needs. I eat "weeds" at almost every home I visit. I want to show my clients what great food Mother Nature has provided at our fingertips. I eat from their yards to help give people a sense that it is normal, it is OK and acceptable and wonderful to eat wild. For most people, this simple matter of having permission from someone is key. Not long ago, a client—a woman and her children—walked me through their garden, abandoned to weeds. I asked about her goals. One goal, she said, was backyard greens for smoothies.

"I was hoping you would say that," I said, picking a handful of purslane. The flavor, I explained as I munched, is like crunchy romaine lettuce with a built-in lemon vinaigrette. I also picked wild spinach (lamb's-quarters), flixweed, clover, and others. She and the kids followed my lead, picking and eating.

"Do you eat like this a lot?" she asked, smiling at the lemony sensation. "You are going to outlive us all."

Introducing people to the vitamin-rich, nutrient-dense, flavorful organic greens, which cost nothing and are already growing at their doorstep, has given me a lot of pleasure over the years. On another occasion, a young family hired me to assess the yard of their new home in the desert. As we walked the property, I picked and ate roughly a dozen weed species, explaining each. The husband tasted them tentatively. Later, in a crowded class I was teaching, the man told my students, "This guy came out to my house and just started eating the weeds. I couldn't believe it—and now I eat them all the time too!" These are the moments teachers live for.

I'm also pleased when no one is impressed when I feast on wild foods. On several occasions I have begun to eat a "weed" in a client's yard, hoping for a reaction of delight and astonishment, only to be told, "Oh yeah, we eat that in our green smoothies every morning." And sometimes clients even introduce wild edibles to me that I didn't know about.

Occasionally, my efforts backfire. A couple years ago, I took a group of people into the Great Basin Desert to explore a cave. When we finished, we decided to go on a short walk to a nearby pond. Along the way, I was picking and eating wild edibles, showing off what the desert had to offer. My eleven-year-old grandson, Xander, who has been eating wild edibles with me since birth, was walking behind me, showing the greens to the kids his age.

Only half paying attention, I peripherally heard him say, "This flower is edible too." But I hadn't shown anyone an edible flower that day, nor had I seen any. Xander had picked a flower that he imagined was edible, but it wasn't. I cautioned him, and he put it down. Xander had seen me eat so many wild things over the years, I think he had gotten the idea in his head that we can eat anything wild. Ever since that day, I have been careful to teach him and everyone that you never, ever put anything into your mouth unless you know with surety the identity of the plant and that it is safe to eat.

While the focus of this book is not on poisonous plants, this story always rings in my memory as a reminder to us all that caution is the rule of the day. A book like this is a starting point. Seeing pictures of a plant does not qualify you to begin wild harvesting. A photograph of a plant records just one moment in time, but the way a plant looks changes every single day of its life cycle, and depends heavily on environmental conditions such as hours of sunlight per day, available water, soil nutrients, seasons, microclimate, and more.

I teach classes in which students are taught to identify wild edibles. If you can't get to one of my classes, find someone in your local area who is an expert. The most dangerous thing you can do is rely on photos from a quick Google search before wandering outside to start picking plants. In my considerable experience, photos of wild edibles online are misidentified at least half of the time. Species-specific online searching is a learned art, and simply typing the scientific name of a plant into the search bar does not work. Most of the time, because of the way search engines work, the pictures are not of the species but the genus. Putting the species name in quote marks can give better results, but the results—especially photos—will still be filled with examples of the genus instead of the species. And almost every plant has a look-alike, and sometimes the look-alikes are deadly poisonous.

However, while caution is important, being immobilized by fear is a mistake. When we go to the grocery store, we don't pause to consider whether a carrot is poisonous or not. This is because we know people who have eaten carrots and not died. We know that carrots are commonly eaten. But somewhere, in the history of the world, there was a day when people did not know whether wild carrots were food or medicine or poison. All the knowledge that we have today about what is edible or not edible comes directly from our ancestors, who experimented to find out. We owe them a debt of gratitude for passing this knowledge to us.

Some of them paid with their lives, but it is important to note that very few plants are deadly poisonous. Most plants that are not edible may just make your stomach upset. When you think about it, our ancestors' experience of learning the hard way what is edible is not as foreign to us as we might want it to be. Today, every day, people put pharmaceutical drugs, chemicals, and manufactured foods in their mouths, thinking they must be safe because they are in stores, only to discover later that the cumulative, long-term effect of these drugs or fake foods results in permanent damage to our bodies. Few people realize there is no government oversight for the long-term effects of what is sold, and testing for long-term effects is not required. In my view, we are all probably much safer eating known wild edibles, filled with beneficial properties, than many of the so-called processed "foods" in the grocery store. Wild edibles, for example, are not going to give you type 2 diabetes—but the vast majority of the stuff on store shelves will.

If you learn just one thing from the book, please let it be this: wild food is for everyday living. Most people think of Mother Nature's buffet as "survival" food—a last resort to be used in a day of need, with fingers crossed that the day will never come. But if you pay quiet, careful attention, you will notice something startling: That day is already here. Pay attention to the number of people around you whose health is deteriorating, who are on an ever-increasing number of pharmaceutical and over-the-counter drugs. Pay attention to the number of people around you whose lives are crippled by autoimmune disorders. As a diabetes and autoimmune nutrition specialist, I see this trend first hand. Everyday I use the principles of correct nutrition to help people come off or reduce insulin to quel its side effects, get off their diabetes medications with their doctor's permission, arrest autoimmune symptoms, lose weight, control blood pressure, and more.

What I know for sure is that what we eat this month will impact our quality of life next year and beyond. There is nothing on Earth as amazing as the human body. The world is filled with the nutrition our bodies need. But nutrition gets harder to find in stores each year. Notice that almost everything in the grocery aisles is a product, not a simple, true food. A

product is created by someone and requires advertising for attention and dollars. True food does not require advertising or fancy packaging or patents or trademarks or intense processing. The products are designed to feed short-term highs, to encourage emotional eating and sugar addiction to benefit corporate coffers. Products encourage our children and their parents to be obese, diabetic, and dependent on pharmaceuticals. Thanks to modern technology, I work with sick people across the nation. I have helped many people save their toes and feet from amputation. For others, I work to prevent further amputation, stroke, tooth loss, and heart attacks. I have a deep knowledge of what food choices do to people. So please let me say once again: natural food is for everyday living. If people would eat a little more from the wild, from gardens, and from the farmers markets, it would change the health of generations. If you or someone you love is sick and don't know how to make the right nutritional changes, get help.

This book is all about natural health. I've written many books on gardening and self-reliance. I've taught thousands of students on the same subjects. I own an heirloom seed company, SeedRensaissance.com (mention any of my books to get free seeds with any paid order). With this book, you can have fun and fall in love with the natural outdoor world all over again while you do it.

Caleb Warnock, August 2019

Abutilon theophrasti

(VELVETLEAF)

U.S.: Found in all states except Alaska and Hawaii.

CANADA: Found in Alberta, British Columbia, Manitoba, New Brunswick, Nova Scotia, Ontario, Prince Edward Island, Quebec, and Saskatchewan.

EDIBLE PARTS: Immature seeds and immature seed pods, which can be cooked or eaten raw. Mature pods and seeds are hard and inedible, so be sure to get them at the soft, immature stage.

WHEN TO HARVEST: Late spring.

FORM: Summer annual growing 3–7 feet tall

HABITAT: Sunny, dry locations.

FLAVOR: Nutty and mild, like wild sunflower seeds.

NOTES: The leaves of velvetleaf are heart-shaped and can grow as large as dinner plates in some cases. Seeds can be up to one-third oil and the leaves are as soft and velvety as the name implies. This plant was reportedly brought to the U.S. in the seventeenth century and grown for its useful fibers used in making cord and cloth. Today's wild population has escaped that cultivation and the plant now has a reputation among campers and survivalists as being useful for emergency toilet paper. The seed pods have an interesting shape that somewhat resembles an origami barrel. The shape of the pods is somewhat reminiscent of garden poppies, with its pleated circular three-dimensional shape. The plant is also sometimes called Chinese jute because the fibers can be used for rope, rough paper, and more. There are even YouTube videos showing how to use the Velvetleaf stalk as the rope for a survivalist hand drill to start a friction fire. Rarely people may have an allergic reaction to the velvet on the leaves.

Acer negundo

(BOX ELDER MAPLE)

U.S.: Found in all states except Alaska and Hawaii.

CANADA: Found in Alberta, British Columbia, Manitoba, New Brunswick, Northwest Territories, Nova Scotia, Ontario, Prince Edward Island, Quebec, and Saskatchewan.

EDIBLE PARTS: Sap of the tree, also called maple water. Boiled or raw.

WHEN TO HARVEST: Spring

FORM: Perennial tree, growing sixty feet tall.

HABITAT: Slopes, mountainsides, plains.

FLOWER COLOR: White or greenish or sometimes pale yellow.

FLAVOR: Slightly sweet.

NOTES: Sap is tapped by wounding the tree in late winter, early spring. Sap is collected in a container and can be used raw but must be clean to be a safe drink. Raw sap is believed by many to have health benefits because of its mineral content. Sap is boiled to make syrup. Sap varies in sugar content by species. *A. saccharum, A. nigrum*, and *A. rubrum* are most sought after because their tsap contains between two percent and five percent sugar and are thus easier to boil down for syrup. But all maples produce drinkable sap. There are numerous online resources that can teach you how to tap maple trees for sap. Timing however is critical. The sap only runs early in the year. In addition to the native varieties listed here, there are many non-native varieties with edible sap that have been widely planted around the Rocky Mountains as landscape trees.

UNIQUE CHARACTERISTICS: This tree hosts boxelder bugs, which many homeowners find to be pests. This tree species is different than most maples in two ways: the tree is either entirely male or entirely female, and it has odd-pinnate compound leaves with three to five toothed leaflets. Leaves turn yellow in autumn. The tree produces weak soft wood. Large limbs can fail in high winds. The seeds are also prolific and viable and can become invasive and sprout many tree seedlings, which need to be removed in the first year or they quickly become difficult to kill and remove.

Achillea millefolium

(WESTERN YARROW)

U.S.: Found in all states.

CANADA: Found in all provinces and territories.

EDIBLE PARTS: Leaves, which are best cooked. Historically it was a popular "pot herb," meaning it was simmered and eaten with other edibles and game meats as a sort of fast food for settlers.

WHEN TO HARVEST: Spring, summer, autumn.

FORM: Perennial plant growing twelve to thirty-six inches tall.

HABITAT: Rocky soils in a wide range of areas including fields, roadsides, meadows, plains, and mountainsides. Grows in both moist and desert areas. Once you learn to recognize this plant, you will begin to see it everywhere.

FLOWER COLOR: White, and sometimes shades of pink.

FLAVOR: Grass-like.

NOTES: Yarrow flower is widely used medicinally and has become especially popular in recent years for tincturing and using in the wild for stings, bites, itching, and other external wounds. The juice of the leaves is used to calm these wounds. Yarrow is sold in health food stores, in dried form and capsules and for medicinal use. Yarrow flowers are striking and drought-hardy and are a favorite for use in xeriscape.

Aegilops cylindrica

(JOINTED GOATGRASS)

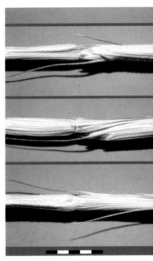

U.S.: Found in all states except Alaska, Connecticut, Delaware, Florida, Georgia, Hawaii, Maine, Maryland, Massachusetts, Minnesota, Mississippi, New Hampshire, New Jersey, North Carolina, Rhode Island, South Carolina, Vermont, and Wisconsin.

CANADA: Not found in Canada.

EDIBLE PARTS: The grain is typically hand-ground to create a course flour, which can be used to make anything you can make with modern flour, including small savory cakes, stew thickener, hard tack for travel, gruel, and more.

WHEN TO HARVEST: Mid-summer.

FORM: Summer annual growing eighteen to twenty-four inches tall.

HABITAT: Open, sunny, and dry disturbed areas such as roadsides, field edges, and sometimes plains.

NOTES: Separating the edible grain from the chaff is difficult, which reduces the usefulness of this grain. Historically, chaff was removed by rubbing the seed heads and then winnowing with the wind. It is my personal belief that historic grains were roughly winnowed, meaning that some chaff was retained and eaten if it could be ground up, and today this would be a useful source of fiber, which is severely lacking in modern food. Fiber is responsible for the pH of the bowel and its absence creates long-term weight and digestive problems. Diets low in fiber have also been repeatedly linked to colon cancer. In other words, we should probably all eat more wild grains and chaff.

Agastache foeniculum

(BLUE GIANT HYSSOP)

U.S.: Found in Alaska, Colorado, Connecticut, Idaho, Illinois, Maine, Michigan, Minnesota, Montana, Nebraska, New Hampshire, New York, North Dakota, Ohio, Pennsylvania, New Jersey, South Dakota, Vermont, Washington, and Wyoming.

CANADA: Found everywhere except Nova Scotia, Nunavut.

EDIBLE PARTS: Leaves and flowers, which can be cooked or eaten raw. However, they have a strong licorice (anise) flavor and so the main use of this plant is for tea and for sparing use in salads as flavoring. Cooking does not significantly reduce the strong flavor.

WHEN TO HARVEST: Mid-summer.

FORM: Summer annual growing eighteen to twenty-four inches tall.

HABITAT: Open, sunny, and dry disturbed areas such as roadsides, field edges, and sometimes plains.

NOTES: This plant, like most hyssop, is a popular perennial garden flower.

Amaranthus Species

U.S.: Found in all states.

CANADA: Found everywhere in Canada except Nunuvat and Yukon territory.

EDIBLE PARTS: The seeds of all *Amaranthus* species are edible; typically they are toasted and ground up as flour, according to Lawrence E. Steckel of the Weed Science Society of America. Most *Amaranthus* also have edible leaves that are best when cooked.

WHEN TO HARVEST: Leaves are harvested from May through August. Seeds are harvested in September and October. Leaves have a mild flavor that is good for salad, green smoothies, or eating raw. One of the benefits of this plant is that the leaves stay tender even when they reach mid-size or larger, so they can be harvested for many weeks. The seeds are harvested after they have naturally dried on the plant in autumn.

FORM: Annual plants ranging from low ground cover to taller aerial weeds.

HABITAT: Open, sunny waste spaces and disturbed earth.

FLOWER COLOR: Varies by species but typically green to pale yellow.

SEED FLAVOR: Grain.

LEAF FLAVOR: Mild grass.

NOTES: Do not assume every species in the genus is edible. Never eat a wild edible unless you have specific information about the species first.

EDIBLE SPECIES EXAMPLES:

Amaranthus albus

  U.S.: Found in all states except Hawaii.

  Canada: Found in Alberta, British Columbia, Manitoba, New Brunswick, Newfoundland and Labrador, Nova Scotia, Ontario, Prince Edward Island, Quebec, and Saskatchewan.

Amarranthus bilotides

  U.S.: Found in all states except Hawaii.

  Canada: Found in Alberta, British Columbia, Manitoba, New Brunswick, Ontario, Quebec, and Saskatchewan.

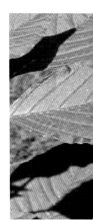

Amaranthus hybridus

U.S.: Found in all states except Alaska, Utah, and Wyoming.

Canada: Found in Manitoba, Nova Scotia, Ontario, and Quebec.

Amaranthus powellii

U.S.: Found in all states except Alabama, Alaska, Delaware, Georgia, Hawaii, Maryland, North Dakota, and Tennessee.

Canada: Found in Alberta, British Columbia, Ontario, Prince Edward Island, Quebec, and Saskatchewan.

Amaranthus retroflexus

U.S.: Found in all states.

Canada: Found in Alberta, British Columbia, Manitoba, New Brunswick, Newfoundland and Labrador, Northwest Territories, Nova Scotia, Ontario, Prince Edward Island, Quebec, and Saskatchewan.

Amaranthus tuberculatus

U.S.: Found in all states except Alaska, Arizona, Hawaii, Maryland, Nevada, Oregon, Utah, and West Virginia.

Canada: Found in Manitoba, Ontario, and Quebec.

Amaranthus tuberculatus

U.S.: Found in all states except Alaska, Arizona, Hawaii, Maryland, Nevada, Oregon, Utah, and West Virginia.

Canada: Found in Manitoba, Ontario, and Quebec.

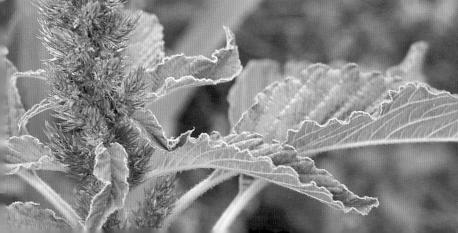

Amaranthus albus

(TUMBLE PIGWEED)

———

See Amaranthus Species for details.

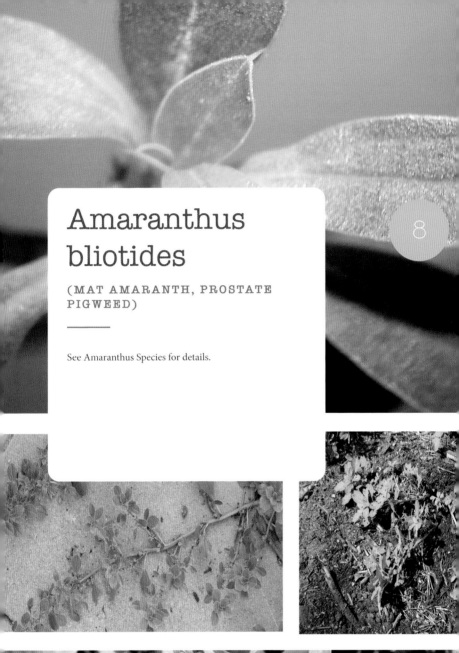

Amaranthus bliotides

(MAT AMARANTH, PROSTATE PIGWEED)

———

See Amaranthus Species for details.

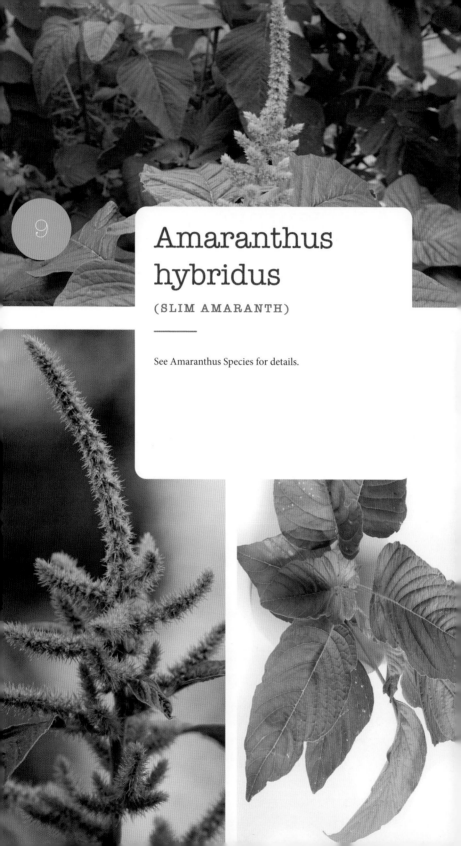

Amaranthus hybridus

(SLIM AMARANTH)

See Amaranthus Species for details.

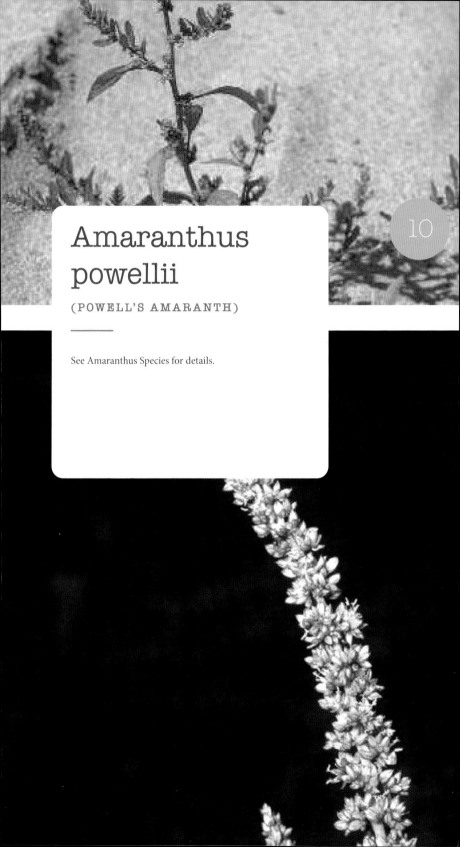

Amaranthus powellii

(POWELL'S AMARANTH)

See Amaranthus Species for details.

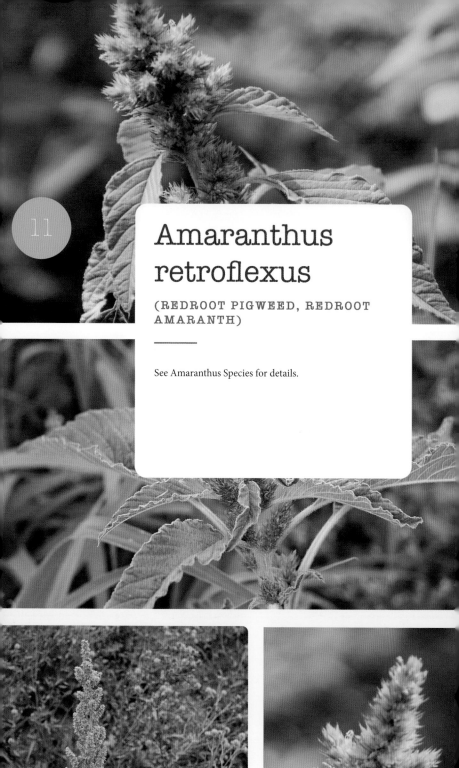

Amaranthus retroflexus

(REDROOT PIGWEED, REDROOT AMARANTH)

See Amaranthus Species for details.

Amaranthus tuberculatus

(ROUGHFRUIT AMARANTH)

———

See Amaranthus Species for details.

Amelanchier alnifolia

(SASKATOON SERVICEBERRY)

U.S.: Found only in north central and northwest states.

CANADA: Found in Alberta, British Columbia, Manitoba, New Brunswick, Northwest Territories, Ontario, Quebec, Saskatchewan, and Yukon.

EDIBLE PARTS: Berries, or leaves for tea. The fruit on all Amelanchier species are edible, according to the U.S. Extension Service.

WHEN TO HARVEST: Late July, August.

FORM: Shrub tree with multiple stems growing five to fifteen feet tall.

HABITAT: Moist shady mountainsides. Commonly found in aspen and maple groves on hiking trails, campgrounds, meadow edges, and creek banks. Prefers to grow in the shade of larger trees.

FLOWER COLOR: White.

BERRY COLOR: Purple.

FLAVOR: Absolutely one of my most favorite wild berries. These have been called mountain blueberries, and with good reason. I actually like them better than blueberries. They are sweet and fleshy and larger than most blueberries from the grocery store. The flavor is fantastic, and for that reason these berry plants are sometimes sold in nurseries for backyard growing. However, this small tree produces well only in shady and humid conditions. Our family harvests them extensively from the mountains, and we also grow them along the shady north side of our barn in an irrigation ditch to fulfill their need for damp soil. The berries change color as they ripen, turning pink and then red, then purple and finally dark purple. For peak

13

ripeness, harvest when the berries are soft and dark purple but before the berries have begun to desiccate. One of the great things about this tree is that the fruit does not all ripen at once, so you can hand-harvest the berries over several weeks. When these berries are in season, I drive to the local canyon weekly to pick them and eat them fresh, on the spot. The berries are irresistible. One downside is that these trees do not produce in prolific amounts. We have even harvested enough to make serviceberry jam, but this required finding a dense grove of trees in the woods.

Articum minus

(LESSER BURDOCK)

_____

U.S.: Found in all states except Alaska, Florida, and Hawaii.

CANADA: Found everywhere except Northwest Territories, Nunavut, and Yukon.

EDIBLE PARTS: Root, leaves, flower stalks, leaf stems.

WHEN TO HARVEST: Spring, summer, autumn.

FORM: Herbaceous biennial growing 2–3 feet tall.

HABITAT: Found widely in calcareous soils in mountains, deserts, residential areas, and roadsides.

FLAVOR: My favorite part of this plant is the stems, which are high in water and have a flavor like celery when they've had good access to water and some shade. Otherwise the stems can be bitter. The young stems can be eaten whole, raw, or cooked. To eat older stems, I usually only scrape out the inside of the stem because the outside is fibrous. The root has a mild and slightly sweet flavor and is easiest to eat when it is thinly sliced. The young leaves have a bitter flavor that is eliminated when cooked.

NOTES: If I were looking for water in the desert, the stems of this plant would be one of the first places I would go to. Burdock is also gaining popularity as a medicinal herb, and I dry the roots for this purpose. Root should be harvested in early summer, before the plant begins to bolt (from flower stalks).

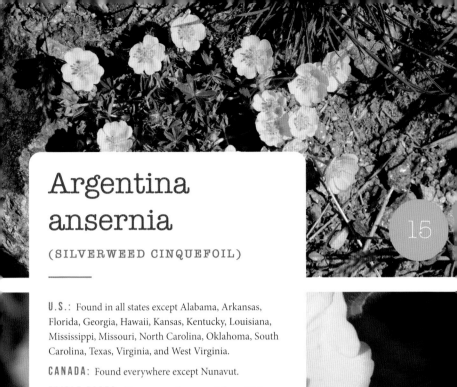

Argentina ansernia

(SILVERWEED CINQUEFOIL)

———

U.S.: Found in all states except Alabama, Arkansas, Florida, Georgia, Hawaii, Kansas, Kentucky, Louisiana, Mississippi, Missouri, North Carolina, Oklahoma, South Carolina, Texas, Virginia, and West Virginia.

CANADA: Found everywhere except Nunavut.

EDIBLE PARTS: The roots and root nodules, which can have a nutty flavor when they are at their peak. The plants often grow in clumps and can produce a bountiful supply of roots and nodules.

WHEN TO HARVEST: Spring, summer, autumn.

FORM: Herbaceous perennial growing 6 inches tall.

HABITAT: Mountainsides.

FLOWER COLOR: Yellow.

FLAVOR: Starchy and nutty, especially in spring. Roots are generally small.

NOTES: This plant produces runners (a trait shared with strawberry plants, which are its cousins) that can make it quite aggressive and invasive in the right conditions. The plant is also used medicinally, but not as commonly as it once was. It is said a poultice of the leaves can have pain-relieving qualities, which certainly deserves more investigation.

15

Artemisia frigida

(FRINGED SAGEBRUSH)

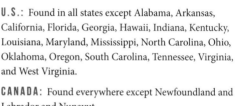

U.S.: Found in all states except Alabama, Arkansas, California, Florida, Georgia, Hawaii, Indiana, Kentucky, Louisiana, Maryland, Mississippi, North Carolina, Ohio, Oklahoma, Oregon, South Carolina, Tennessee, Virginia, and West Virginia.

CANADA: Found everywhere except Newfoundland and Labrador and Nunavut.

EDIBLE PARTS: Leaves used as a condiment for flavoring.

WHEN TO HARVEST: Spring, summer, autumn.

FORM: Shrub typically three to four feet tall.

HABITAT: Desert, alkaline soils.

FLOWER COLOR: Yellow.

FLAVOR: The leaves have a strong spearmint gum flavor that can be useful for bringing moisture to your mouth on a hot day or if you are thirsty, but the strong flavor makes it less useful for food. A tiny bit of leaf goes a long way. Some people use the leaves to make a simple sauce or as a garnish for lamb or pork. To me, this makes the food taste like chewing gum, but some people like it.

Ascelpias
Species

EDIBLE PARTS: Flowers; unopened flower buds; seeds; immature seed pods; brown sugar from flowers, roots, and young sprouts.

WHEN TO HARVEST: July, August, September.

FORM: Native herbaceous perennial or annual, typically two to five feet tall.

HABITAT: Disturbed sunny locations, especially roadsides and field edges.

FLOWER COLOR: Pink upper petals with dark pink to red lower petals, with exotic color variations by species ranging from greens to pinks, reds to purples, and even splotches of black.

FLAVOR: The flowers, buds, and young pods have a delicious sugary flavor that is both a surprise and a treat. Eat just the flowers and not the flower stems to avoid the milk of the plant. I pop the flowerheads off one at a time. The young flower pods delightfully pop in your mouth when eaten. However, flowers and other parts of the plant that are not young and tender may have a bitter flavor. Some species of butterfly are said to depend on these plants for food, so you may want to harvest sparingly. Tender shoots of the plant are eaten like asparagus in early spring, but this decimates the year's crop, so this use may be best sparingly.

OTHER USES: The mature, cottony down of the seed pods has been widely used as a cotton-like stuffing for mattresses, cloth dolls, pillows, and more, especially in times when cotton was expensive or unavailable. The down is also useful as tinder for starting fires from sparks and can be gathered and stored for this purpose. Various parts of the plant also have medicinal uses. Milkweed is also a dye plant. The dry seed pods naturally split on their own and are a favorite toy boat for children. A type of paper can be made from the processed fiber of the stalks. A type of rubber can be made from the milk of the plant, but people may have a skin contact allergy to the milk.

NOTE: This plant may be high in alkaloids and, like all plants in this book, should be eaten sparingly. Avoid eating the milky sap. Do not assume every species in the genus is edible. Never eat a wild edible unless you have specific information about the species first.

EDIBLE SPECIES EXAMPLES:

Ascelpias incarnata

U.S.: Found in all states except Alaska, Arizona, California, Hawaii, Mississippi, Oregon, and Washington.

Canada: Found in Manitoba, New Brunswick, Nova Scotia, Ontario, Prince Edward Island, and Quebec.

Asclepias syrica

U.S.: Found in all states except Alaska, Arizona, California, Colorado, Florida, Hawaii, Idaho, Nevada, New Mexico, Utah, Washington, and Wyoming.

Canada: Found in Manitoba, New Brunswick, Nova Scotia, Ontario, Prince Edward Island, Quebec, and Saskatchewan.

Asclepias verticillata

U.S.: Found in all states except Alaska, California, Colorado, Hawaii, Idaho, Maine, Nevada, New Hampshire, Oregon, Utah, and Washington.

Canada: Found in Manitoba, Ontario, and Saskatchewan.

Asclepias verticillata

U.S.: Found in all states except Alaska, California, Hawaii, Idaho, Maine, Massachusetts, Nevada, New Hampshire, Oregon, Rhode Island, Utah, Vermont, and Washington.

Canada: Found in Alberta, British Columbia, Manitoba, Ontario, and Saskatchewan.

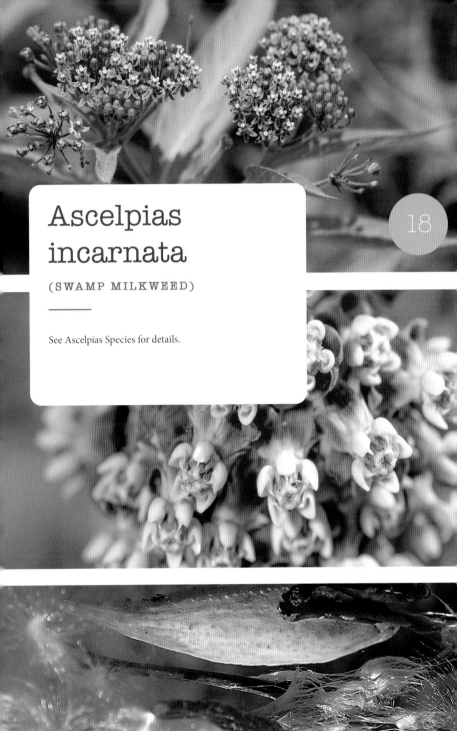

Ascelpias
incarnata

(SWAMP MILKWEED)

See Ascelpias Species for details.

18

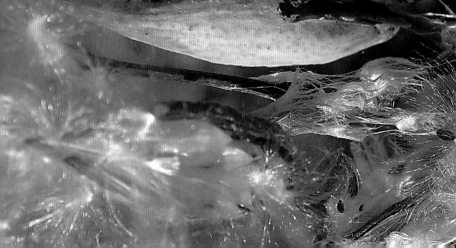

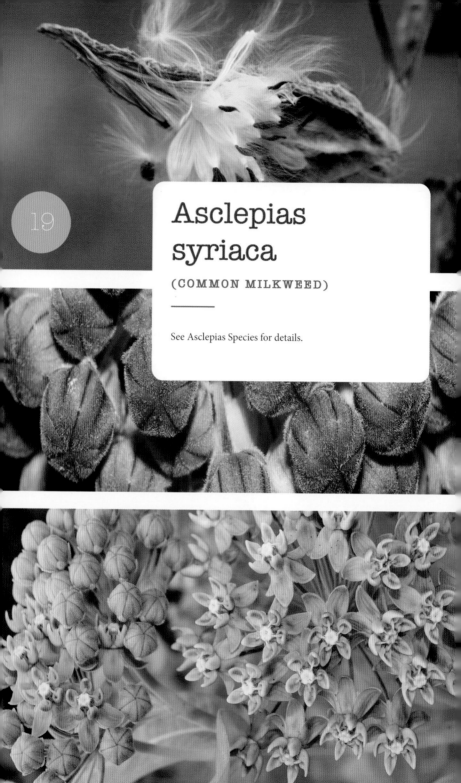

Asclepias syriaca

(COMMON MILKWEED)

See Asclepias Species for details.

Asclepias
verticillata

(WHORLED MILKWEED)

———————

See Asclepias Species for details.

Asclepias viridiflora

(GREEN COMET MILKWEED)

See Asclepias Species for details.

Avena Species

EDIBLE PARTS: Grain. All Avena species have edible seeds. Can be ground for flour, soaked, sprouted, boiled, added to soup, used in multi-grain bread, and used with natural baking yeast. (For recipes and instructions on natural baking yeast, see *The Art of Baking with Natural Yeast*.)

WHEN TO HARVEST: July, August, September.

FORM: Annual, two feet tall, grass-like plant.

HABITAT: Found in disturbed and somewhat dry areas in heavy clay soil, and sometimes in drier meadows.

FLAVOR: Grain.

NOTES: Oats are easy to grow and mature rapidly, making them one of the fastest grains to grow from scratch. Even the straw is useful as garden compost and in garden pathways.

EDIBLE SPECIES EXAMPLES:

Avena fatua

   U.S.: Found in all states except Arkansas, Georgia, North Carolina, and South Carolina.

   CANADA: Found everywhere except Newfoundland and Labrador, Nunavut, and Yukon.

Avena sativa

   U.S.: Found in all states.

   CANADA: Found everywhere except Newfoundland and Labrador and Nunavut.

Avena fatua

(WILD OAT)

See Avena Species for details.

Avena sativa

(COMMON OAT)

———

See Avena Species for details.

24

Barbarea Species

EDIBLE PARTS: Leaves.

WHEN TO HARVEST: Spring, summer, autumn.

FORM: Herbaceous native perennial up to two feet tall.

HABITAT: Wet soils, especially along streams and creeks.

FLOWER COLOR: Yellow.

FLAVOR: Spicy hot when raw; somewhat calmer when cooked.

NOTES: Edible oil can be extracted from the crushed seed. Like many members of the mustard family, both species listed here have clusters of bright yellow flowers in late spring that really bring color to the garden. We like to bring them indoors as cut flowers, where they last up to two weeks. They have a way of cheering up any space, indoor or out.

EDIBLE SPECIES EXAMPLES:

Barbarea vulgaris

> **U.S.:** Found in all states except Alaska, Arizona, Hawaii, Louisiana, Mississippi, Nevada, and Texas.
>
> **CANADA:** Found everywhere except Northwest Territories, Nunavut, and Yukon.

Barbarea othoceras

> **U.S.:** Not found in United States.
>
> **CANADA:** Found everywhere except Nova Scotia, Nunavut, and Prince Edward Island.

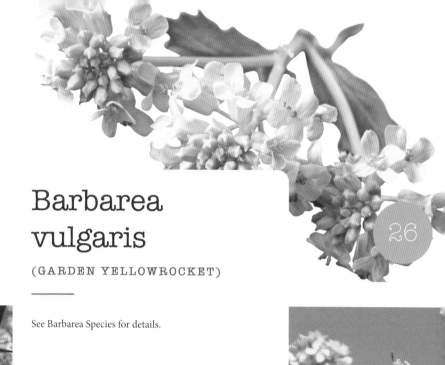

Barbarea vulgaris

(GARDEN YELLOWROCKET)

See Barbarea Species for details.

Barbarea othoceras

(AMERICAN YELLOWROCKET)

See Barbarea Species for details.

27

Brassica Species

EDIBLE PARTS: Flowers, leaves, root, seed.

WHEN TO HARVEST: Spring, summer, autumn.

FORM: Herbaceous annual growing three to four feet tall.

HABITAT: Heavy disturbed clay soils.

FLOWER COLOR: Yellow.

FLAVOR: Wild Brassicas typically have a peppery flavor unless they are picked quite young or in ideal moisture and heat conditions. The flavor is improved by cooking for even just a couple of minutes.

NOTES: In addition to their wild forms, *B. rapa* and *B. juncea* both have sibling varieties that are commonly grown as vegetables, including Asian salad greens like Chinese cabbage, Mizuna, Osaka purple mustard, broccoli, cauliflower, kale, cabbage, and more. You can purchase seeds for many *Brassica* vegetables at my website, SeedRenaissance.com. There are more than four thousand *Brassica* species. Do not assume every species in the genus is edible. Never eat a wild edible unless you have specific information about the species first.

EDIBLE SPECIES EXAMPLES:

Brassica juncea

> **U.S.:** Found in all states.
>
> **CANADA:** Found everywhere except Newfoundland and Labrador, Nunavut, and Yukon.

Brassica napus

> **U.S.:** Found in all states except Arizona, Florida, Hawaii, Minnesota, Nebraska, North Dakota, Pennsylvania, South Dakota, Texas, Utah, and Wyoming.
>
> **CANADA:** Found everywhere except Nunavut and Yukon.

Brassica nigra

> **U.S.:** Found in all states except Alaska, Arkansas, Georgia, South Carolina, and Wyoming.
>
> **CANADA:** Found everywhere except Newfoundland and Labrador, Northwest Territories, Nunavut, and Yukon.

Brassica rapa

> **U.S.:** Found in all states.
>
> **CANADA:** Found everywhere except Nunavut.

29

Brassica juncea

(BROWN MUSTARD)

See Brassica Species for details.

Brassica napus

(RAPE MUSTARD)

———

See Brassica Species for details.

Brassica nigra

(BLACK MUSTARD)

See Brassica Species for details.

Brassica rapa

(FIELD MUSTARD)

———

See Brassica Species for details.

Bromus Species

U.S.: Found in all states.

CANADA: Found in all provinces and territories.

EDIBLE PARTS: Mature seeds are harvested and boiled whole after removing the chaff by rubbing or ground into flour after winnowing using the wind. I even chew on the immature milky seeds when hiking.

WHEN TO HARVEST: Summer, autumn.

FORM: Annual invasive grass that relies on early spring moisture for germination.

HABITAT: Dryland open slopes, plains, roadsides, and disturbed areas.

FLAVOR: Nutty grain.

NOTES: *B. marginatusis,* in some but not all expert opinions, a synonym for *B. breviaristatus.*

EDIBLE SPECIES EXAMPLES:

Bromus japonicus

> **U.S.:** Found in all states except Alaska and Hawaii.
>
> **CANADA:** Found everywhere except in New Brunswick, Newfoundland and Labrador, Northwest Territories, Nova Scotia, Nunavut, Prince Edward Island, and Yukon.

Bromus secalinus

> **U.S.:** Found in all states except North Dakota.
>
> **CANADA:** Found everywhere except Manitoba, Newfoundland and Labrador, Northwest Territories, Nunavut, Ontario, and Saskatchewan.
>
> **CANADA:** Found everywhere except Nunavut and Yukon.

Bromus tectorum

> **U.S.:** Found in all states.
>
> **CANADA:** Found everywhere except Newfoundland and Labrador and Nunavut. Labrador, Northwest Territories, Nunavut, and Yukon.

Brassica rapa

> **U.S.:** Found in all states.

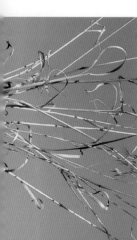

Bromus japonicus

(JAPANESE BROME, FIELD BROME)

———

See Bromus Species for details.

34

Bromus secalinus

(CHEAT, RYE BROME)

See Bromus Species for details.

Bromus tectorum

(DOWNY BROME, CHEAT GRASS)

See Bromus Species for details.

Calypso bulbosa

(FAIRY SLIPPER)

———

U.S.: Not found in United States.

CANADA: Found everywhere except Newfoundland and Labrador.

EDIBLE PARTS: Root.

FLOWER COLOR: Pink, purple.

FORM: Small perennial herbaceous flower.

HABITAT: Moist, shady alkaline soil.

FLAVOR: Buttery flavor root, especially in spring.

NOTES: Not widely found, and usually not recommended for harvest because it is scarce. Part of the reason this flower is not widely found is that it is hemi-mycoheterotrophic, which means it is symbiotic with a specific fungus, relying on the underground plant to provide part of its nutrients. The Lady Bird Johnson Wildflower Center says the genus name comes from the *Odyssey's* sea nymph Calypso, "who detained the willing Odysseus on his return from Troy; like Calypso, the plant is beautiful and prefers secluded haunts."

Calystegia sepium

(HEDGE BINDWEED)

———————

U.S.: Found in all states except Hawaii.

CANADA: Found everywhere except Newfoundland and Labrador, Northwest Territories, Nunavut, and Yukon.

EDIBLE PARTS: Leaves, root, stalks, shoots; all should be eaten only in small amounts.

FLOWER COLOR: White, sometimes blushing pink or purple.

FORM: Annual twining vine has funnel-shaped flowers; this plant resembles but is not related to morning glory.

HABITAT: Moist soil including lawns, gardens, roadsides, mountainsides.

FLAVOR: Mild, lightly sweet.

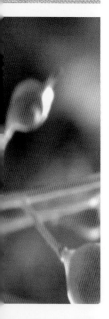

Camelina Species

EDIBLE PARTS: Seeds.

WHEN TO HARVEST: August, September.

FLOWER COLOR: Yellow.

FORM: Annual growing 1–3 feet tall with branched stems.

HABITAT: Full sun, tolerates a wide range of soils and conditions.

FLAVOR: A nutty, slightly oily flavor.

NOTES: We grow *C. sativa* in our garden as a grain for home use. *Camelina* is being touted as the next quinoa, a healthy grain that deserves to be more widely eaten because it is high in protein and natural omega-3 fatty acids. Beyond health benefits and flavor, *Camelina* has two other hugely important assets—it is one of the easiest grains in the world to harvest and clean because the inflated pods break open easily when dried and contain lots of seeds. The pods are easily separated from the grain, even by sieve. There is no manual rubbing or cleaning necessary, as is required with wheat, oats, barley, and other common grains. Lastly, the grain grows well in rich or poor soils, so it can be sowed in the family garden or in heavy clay soil. The seeds can be planted in late fall for spring germination, or even in early spring, and only need to be lightly raked into the soil. In some areas, these plants may be dry-farmed, meaning they don't need additional water. The plants can be grown thickly to maximize the grain harvest. Camelina seeds are available at SeedRenaissance.com. The seeds are thirty to forty percent oil and fourty percent protein according to the National Resource Conservation Center Plant Guide.

EDIBLE SPECIES EXAMPLES:

Camelina microcarpa

U.S.: Found in all states except Alabama, Alaska, Florida, and Hawaii.

CANADA: Found everywhere except Newfoundland and Labrador, Northwest Territories, and Nunavut.

Camelina sativa

U.S.: Found in all states except Alabama, Arkansas, California, Colorado, Florida, Georgia, Hawaii, Indiana, Mississippi, Nevada, Tennessee, and Texas.

CANADA: Found everywhere except Newfoundland and Labrador, Nunavut, and Prince Edward Island.

Camelina microcarpa

(LESSER GOLD OF PLEASURE)

See Camelina Species for details.

Camelina sativa

(GOLD OF PLEASURE)

———

See Camelina Species for details.

Campanula rapunculoides

(CREEPING BELLFLOWER)

U.S.: Found in all states except Alabama, Arizona, Arkansas, California, Florida, Georgia, Hawaii, Louisiana, Mississippi, Oklahoma, and South Carolina.

CANADA: Found everywhere except Newfoundland and Labrador, Northwest Territories, Nunavut, and Yukon.

EDIBLE PARTS: Leaves, root, flower.

WHEN TO HARVEST: July, August.

FLOWER COLOR: Purple.

FORM: Spreading herbaceous perennial flower that can grow five feet tall.

HABITAT: Prefers shade in dry areas .

FLAVOR: Mild, pleasant. Roots have a slight sweetness.

NOTES: We grow this plant in our yard as a beautiful, showy July landscaping flower. The plants include spikes with two feet of purple flowers. These flowers are drought tolerant and will colonize an area if given regular water, making them a good, tall choice for the back of perennial flower beds. The leaves are best before the flowers open; afterward, they get somewhat tough. Plants that get regular water taste better than plants tolerating drought. Seeds are available at SeedRenaissance.com.

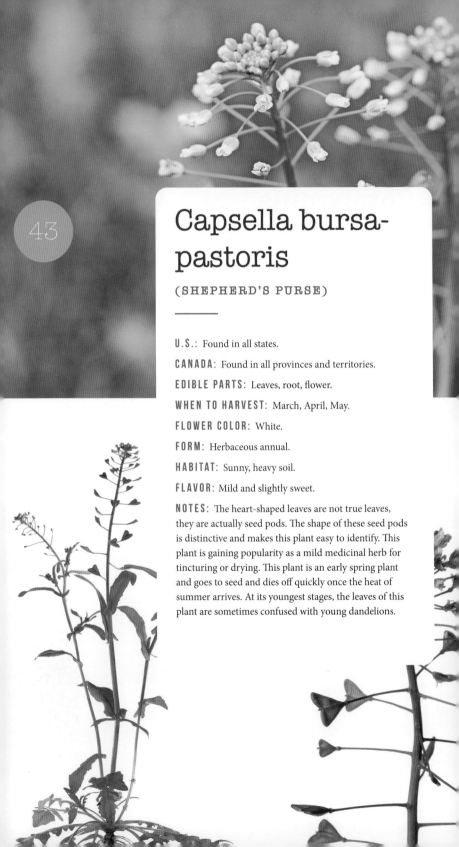

Capsella bursa-pastoris

(SHEPHERD'S PURSE)

———

U.S.: Found in all states.

CANADA: Found in all provinces and territories.

EDIBLE PARTS: Leaves, root, flower.

WHEN TO HARVEST: March, April, May.

FLOWER COLOR: White.

FORM: Herbaceous annual.

HABITAT: Sunny, heavy soil.

FLAVOR: Mild and slightly sweet.

NOTES: The heart-shaped leaves are not true leaves, they are actually seed pods. The shape of these seed pods is distinctive and makes this plant easy to identify. This plant is gaining popularity as a mild medicinal herb for tincturing or drying. This plant is an early spring plant and goes to seed and dies off quickly once the heat of summer arrives. At its youngest stages, the leaves of this plant are sometimes confused with young dandelions.

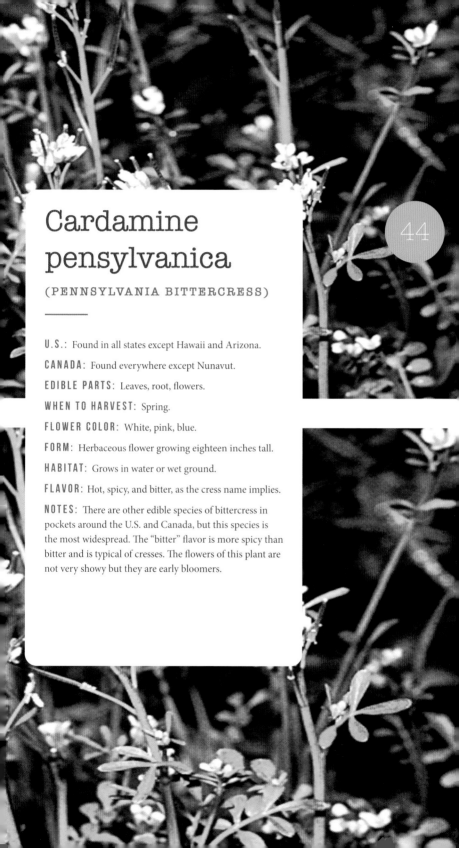

Cardamine pensylvanica

(PENNSYLVANIA BITTERCRESS)

———————

U.S.: Found in all states except Hawaii and Arizona.

CANADA: Found everywhere except Nunavut.

EDIBLE PARTS: Leaves, root, flowers.

WHEN TO HARVEST: Spring.

FLOWER COLOR: White, pink, blue.

FORM: Herbaceous flower growing eighteen inches tall.

HABITAT: Grows in water or wet ground.

FLAVOR: Hot, spicy, and bitter, as the cress name implies.

NOTES: There are other edible species of bittercress in pockets around the U.S. and Canada, but this species is the most widespread. The "bitter" flavor is more spicy than bitter and is typical of cresses. The flowers of this plant are not very showy but they are early bloomers.

44

Cardaria draba

(WHITETOP, HOARY CRESS)

U.S.: Found in all states except Alabama, Alaska, Arkansas, Florida, Georgia, Hawaii, Louisiana, Mississippi, North Carolina, South Carolina, and Tennessee.

CANADA: Found everywhere except Newfoundland and Labrador, Northwest Territories, Nunavut, and Yukon.

EDIBLE PARTS: Leaves, seeds.

WHEN TO HARVEST: Spring.

FLOWER COLOR: White.

FORM: Herbaceous perennial flower growing up to twenty-four inches tall. It is not unusual for this plant to form large masses along roadsides and ditches, and when in bloom, the whole area becomes a solid mass of snowy white flowers. Farmers find this aggressive plant to be a particular nuisance.

HABITAT: Roadsides, ditch banks, fields.

FLAVOR: Spicy radish or cress flavor. The seeds are used as a pepper substitute.

NOTES: This plant is commonly found growing thickly on roadsides and ditch banks in spring, but harvesting from any place where the plants may have been exposed to pesticides, herbicides, or car exhaust is not recommended—and farmers often target this plant for spraying on field edges and roadsides because, left uncontrolled, it is aggressive. Because this plant is so spicy, it is not one of my favorites, but people who love horseradish often love this vegetable.

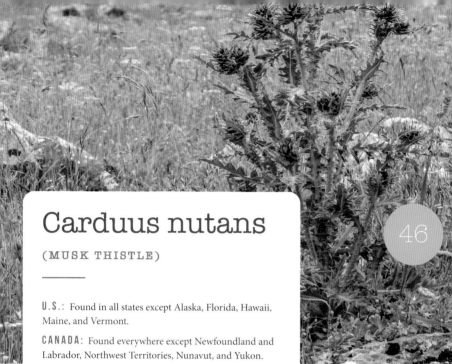

Carduus nutans

(MUSK THISTLE)

U.S.: Found in all states except Alaska, Florida, Hawaii, Maine, and Vermont.

CANADA: Found everywhere except Newfoundland and Labrador, Northwest Territories, Nunavut, and Yukon.

EDIBLE PARTS: The pith of the stems can be eaten boiled. The young flower is used as milk rennet.

FLOWER COLOR: Purple.

FORM: One to seven spiny branched stems growing up to 6 feet tall.

HABITAT: Open spaces, disturbed soil.

FLAVOR: Mild.

NOTES: The flowers of this and most large purple-flowered thistles can be used to curdle milk for making soft cheeses at home (see below for homemade soft cheese recipe). For hard cheese and other recipes and information, see my book Make Your Own Cheese with twelve cheese recipes.

MUSK THISTLE CHEESE

1 musk thistle flowerheads

1 gallon milk

The flowerhead is picked just as the petals begin to appear, before the flower opens. Rinse and place flowerheads in a gallon of milk and leave at room temperature until the milk has turned thick and begun to separate into curds and whey. Remove flowerheads. Line a sieve with a straining cloth. Pour curd and whey into the sieve and allow whey to drain into a bowl. When the whey is drained, the condensed curd that remains in the sieve is a soft cheese that can be used immediately or refrigerated for several days.

Carum carvi

(COMMON CARAWAY)

U.S.: Found in all states except Alabama, Alaska, Arizona, Arkansas, California, Florida, Georgia, Hawaii, Kansas, Mississippi, Nebraska, Nevada, Oklahoma, South Carolina, and Texas.

CANADA: Found everywhere except Newfoundland and Labrador, Northwest Territories, Nunavut, and Yukon.

EDIBLE PARTS: Leaves, root, seed.

WHEN TO HARVEST: Root is best in the first year. Leaves are best when young and tender.

FLOWER COLOR: White.

FORM: Biennial flower growing up to four feet tall.

HABITAT: Fields, roadsides, disturbed soil

FLAVOR: Aromatic.

NOTES: This is the common spice that is sold in grocery stores worldwide. It is easy to grow in the home garden. Archeological digs have proven that caraway has been used as a spice for thousands of years, and the seeds were also used to make savory breads. The seeds are also used to help fight heartburn and the oil is used as an expectorant.

Celtis occidentalis

(COMMON HACKBERRY)

U.S.: Found in all states except Alaska, Arizona, California, Hawaii, Idaho, Louisiana, Maine, Nevada, Oregon, and Washington.

CANADA: Found in Manitoba, Ontario, and Quebec.

EDIBLE PARTS: Berry-sized fruit.

WHEN TO HARVEST: Early autumn.

FLOWER COLOR: Green and white.

FORM: Tree, growing up to eighty feet tall.

HABITAT: Sandy or rocky soils near water.

FLAVOR: Sweet.

BERRY COLOR: Brown, red, orange, black, or purple depending on location, condition, and subspecies.

NOTES: There are about sixty species of *Celtis* and most of them are edible. This tree grows as a shrub, small tree, or huge tree depending on conditions and species. Hackberry trees prefer locations with access to water, and grows larger in those locations. While the flavor is good, the problem with hackberries is that each berry is a thin amount of flesh around a large pit; otherwise, they might be sold commercially. The berries are hard and are best used as jam (see below for homemade jam recipe).

HACKBERRY FREEZER JAM

(makes 1 cup of jam)

2 cups fully ripe dark red hackberries

½ cup sugar or Pyure stevia

Water

Rinse berries and place in a saucepan. You can remove the stems but you don't have to. Cover with water and simmer 30 minutes. Remove from heat and strain out pits/stems using a colander. Remove as much fruit pulp as you easily can from the colander and add it back into the strained liquid. Discard the leftovers in the colander. Add sugar to liquid and bring to a boil for 1 minute. Cool and serve, refrigerate for 1–2 weeks, or freeze for up to six months.

Cenchrus longispinus

(LONGSPINE SANDBUR)

U.S.: Found in all states except Alaska, Hawaii, and Idaho.

CANADA: Found in British Columbia, Ontario, and Quebec.

EDIBLE PARTS: Seeds.

WHEN TO HARVEST: Summer, autumn.

FLOWER COLOR: Green.

FORM: Spiny, spreading, low-growing grass.

HABITAT: Heavy, disturbed soils, roadsides, fields.

FLAVOR: Mild.

NOTES: Inside each horrible puncture burr are one to three tiny edible seeds. It seems to me that when a plant is as hated as this one is, our best revenge is to feast upon it. However, feast carefully because to get to the seeds you have to go through the burs. This plant is extra horrible because research has shown that some of the seeds germinate the first year, and others germinate in later years, making this painful plant extra hard to eradicate. Use leather gloves to harvest. Crush the burrs to get to the seeds, but don't use your hands to do this or you may get barbs. Do not eat unless you are 100 percent sure you have removed all barbs and have only seeds.

Centaurea cyanus

(GARDEN CORNFLOWER)

U.S.: Found in all states except Alaska.

CANADA: Found everywhere except Newfoundland and Labrador, Northwest Territories, Nunavut, and Saskatchewan.

EDIBLE PARTS: Flower.

WHEN TO HARVEST: Early summer.

FLOWER COLOR: Blue (*C. cyanus*); pink, purple or pale blue (*C. jacea*). Natural hybrids are the cause of some of the flower color variety.

FORM: Slender annual flower typically two to three feet tall.

HABITAT: Roadsides, plains, meadows.

FLAVOR: Mild, slightly sweet cucumber flavor.

NOTES: Dried flower petals of *C. cyanus* are sold to make a tea that is a widely used medicinal. An edible blue dye can be made from the flower of *C. cyanus*. Many colors of hybrid cornflower are available but wild plants have only blue flowers. The flowers are common salad garnishes. The flowers are also long-lasting in a vase for display. The flowers look similar to chicory flowers.

Chamerion Species

EDIBLE PARTS: Flowers, leaves, root, stem.

WHEN TO HARVEST: Summer.

FLOWER COLOR: Red/Purple.

FORM: Slender showy flower growing up to five feet tall.

HABITAT: Mountains near water.

FLAVOR: Mild.

NOTES: I often eat the leaves when hiking in summer. They are pleasant and more substantial than most greens. The flowers also have a mild flavor and are fun to pop in your mouth as you walk along a trail. *Epilobium latifolium* is a synonym for "dwarf fireweed." *Epilobium angustifolium* is a synonym for "fireweed." Kids also think it is fun to eat them while hiking.

EDIBLE SPECIES EXAMPLES:

Chamerion angustifolium

> **U.S.:** Found in all states except Alabama, Arkansas, Florida, Georgia, Hawaii, Kansas, Kentucky, Louisiana, Mississippi, Missouri, Oklahoma, South Carolina, and Texas.

> **CANADA:** Found in all provinces and territories.

Chamerion latifolium

> **U.S.:** Not found in United States.

> **CANADA:** Found everywhere except New Brunswick, Nova Scotia, Prince Edward Island, and Saskatchewan.

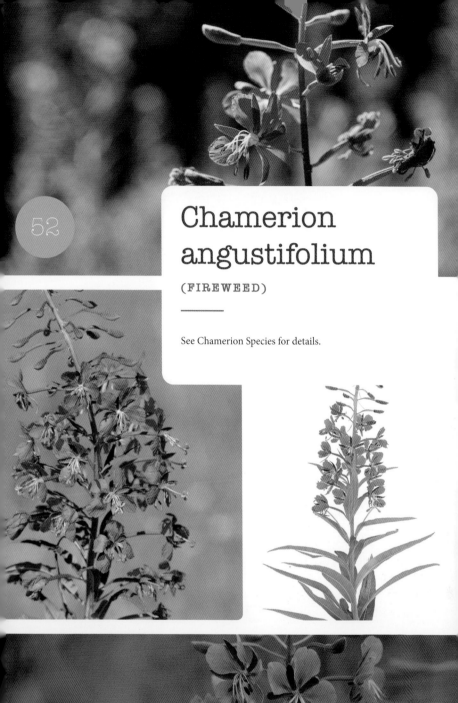

Chamerion angustifolium

(FIREWEED)

—

See Chamerion Species for details.

Chamerion latifolium

(DWARF FIREWEED)

———

See Chamerion Species for details.

Chenopodium Species

U.S.: Found in all states.

CANADA: Found everywhere except Nunavut.

EDIBLE PARTS: Leaves, seeds.

WHEN TO HARVEST: Spring, summer.

FLOWER COLOR: Green.

FORM: Herbaceous plant typically growing four to five feet tall.

HABITAT: Sunny open spaces in heavy soils.

FLAVOR: Mild.

NOTES: Lamb's-quarter is one of the wild greens I eat the most, simply because it grows so prolifically on our property. In the wild it is found at many elevations and tastes best before bolting to flower in summer, but even bitter summer leaves are made pleasant by cooking or blanching. I mostly eat this raw while gardening or hiking. A prolific producer, easy to find, with good mild flavor. Do not assume every species in the genus is edible. Never eat a wild edible unless you have specific information about the species first.

EDIBLE SPECIES EXAMPLES:

Chenopodium album

   U.S.: Found in all states.

   CANADA: Found everywhere except Nunavut.

Chenopodium berlandierie

   U.S.: Found in all states except Hawaii.

   CANADA: Found everywhere except Newfoundland and Labrador and Nunavut.

Chenopodium murale

   U.S.: Found in all states except Alaska, Colorado, Louisiana, Minnesota, Nebraska, North Dakota, and South Dakota.

   CANADA: Found in New Brunswick, Ontario, Quebec, and Saskatchewan.

Chenopodium album

(LAMB'S-QUARTERS, WILD SPINACH)

———

See Chenopodium Species for details.

Chenopodium berlandieri

(GOOSEFOOT, NETSEED LAMB'S QUARTERS)

See Chenopodium Species for details.

Chenopodium murale

(NETTLELEAF GOOSEFOOT)

See Chenopodium Species for details.

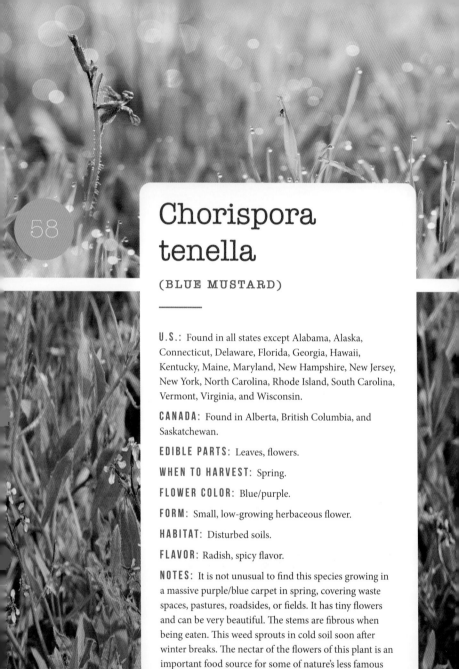

Chorispora tenella

(BLUE MUSTARD)

U.S.: Found in all states except Alabama, Alaska, Connecticut, Delaware, Florida, Georgia, Hawaii, Kentucky, Maine, Maryland, New Hampshire, New Jersey, New York, North Carolina, Rhode Island, South Carolina, Vermont, Virginia, and Wisconsin.

CANADA: Found in Alberta, British Columbia, and Saskatchewan.

EDIBLE PARTS: Leaves, flowers.

WHEN TO HARVEST: Spring.

FLOWER COLOR: Blue/purple.

FORM: Small, low-growing herbaceous flower.

HABITAT: Disturbed soils.

FLAVOR: Radish, spicy flavor.

NOTES: It is not unusual to find this species growing in a massive purple/blue carpet in spring, covering waste spaces, pastures, roadsides, or fields. It has tiny flowers and can be very beautiful. The stems are fibrous when being eaten. This weed sprouts in cold soil soon after winter breaks. The nectar of the flowers of this plant is an important food source for some of nature's less famous pollinators, including long-tongued bees, bee flies, skippers, and moths.

Cichorium intybus

(CHICORY)

U.S.: Found in all states except Alaska and Hawaii.

CANADA: Found everywhere except Northwest Territories, Nunavut, and Yukon.

EDIBLE PARTS: Root, leaves.

WHEN TO HARVEST: Spring, summer.

FLOWER COLOR: Blue.

FORM: Slender, wiry flower typically growing three feet tall.

HABITAT: Disturbed soils in sunny, dry locations.

FLAVOR: The leaves have a mild flavor. The root has a grass-like flavor with a mildly bitter aftertaste, especially when it has been exposed to drought.

NOTES: Flowers are edible but bitter; root tastes best roasted. Flowers open until noon. Inulin is found in roots and is naturally sweet and good for glycemic index and is found in many commercial yogurts. Inulin is a prebiotic fiber. This plant has infested our backyard pasture and is almost impossible to get rid of. It is extremely drought-tolerant. The stalks of the plant can be almost wiry and the fiber has been used to make rope, paper, and fabric. The flowers can be stunningly beautiful in the morning sun. Chicory plants can also be "sprouted" in a winter root cellar to produce salad greens, an ancient practice going back centuries. The lack of light blanches the young leaf sprouts and they have a good flavor—and it's fun to grow blanched "greens" in the middle of winter.

Cirsium Species

U.S.: Found in all states.

CANADA: Found everywhere except Newfoundland and Labrador, Nunavut, and Yukon territory.

EDIBLE PARTS: Roots of first year, leaves minus spines, stems peeled, leaves curdle milk.

WHEN TO HARVEST: Spring, summer.

FLOWER COLOR: Purple.

FORM: Spreading, branching spiny stems growing up to seven feet tall.

HABITAT: Strongly invasive in disturbed soil, wastelands, and roadsides.

FLAVOR: Lemony.

NOTES: Seeds can be roasted for eating. Thistle down is easily lit by a flint and steel and makes excellent fire-starting tinder. The flower head, picked just as the petals begin to open, can be rinsed and used to curdle milk to make cheese. See recipe under "Musk Thistle." Canada thistle actually has no relation to Canada, and understandably Canada is not happy to be "blamed" for the existence of this aggressive weed. These species are also sometimes called "cursed thistle" by farmers because if you plow them up, the plow simply breaks up the roots and each root piece sprouts a new plant. Do not assume every species in the genus is edible. Never eat a wild edible unless you have specific information about the species first.

EDIBLE SPECIES EXAMPLES:

Cirsium arvense

> **U.S.:** Found in all states except Georgia, Hawaii, Louisiana, Mississippi, Oklahoma, South Carolina, and Texas.
>
> **CANADA:** Found everywhere except Newfoundland and Labrador and Nunavut.

Cirsium vulgare

> **U.S.:** Found in all states.
>
> **CANADA:** Found everywhere except Newfoundland and Labrador, Nunavut, and Yukon.

Chenopodium murale

> **U.S.:** Found in all states except Alaska, Colorado, Louisiana, Minnesota, Nebraska, North Dakota, and South Dakota.
>
> **CANADA:** Found in New Brunswick, Ontario, Quebec, and Saskatchewan.

Cirsium arvense

(CANADA THISTLE)

See Cirsium Species for details.

Cirsium vulgare

(COMMON THISTLE, BULL THISTLE)

See Cirsium Species for details.

Cleome serrulata

(ROCKY MOUNTAIN BEE PLANT)

———————

U.S.: Found in all states except Alabama, Alaska, Arkansas, Delaware, Florida, Georgia, Hawaii, Kentucky, Louisiana, Maryland, Mississippi, New Hampshire, New Jersey, North Carolina, Pennsylvania, South Carolina, Tennessee, Vermont, Virginia, and West Virginia.

CANADA: Found in Alberta, British Columbia, Manitoba, Ontario, Quebec, and Saskatchewan.

EDIBLE PARTS: Petals, leaves, seeds, seedpods.

WHEN TO HARVEST: Summer.

FLOWER COLOR: Purple.

FORM: Branching stemmed flower growing up to 4 feet tall.

HABITAT: Wastelands, roadsides in open sunny locations.

FLAVOR: Hot.

NOTES: One of the most beautiful of all wildflowers of the West. This is a huge, showy plant in August that definitely should be grown more as a landscape plant. Seeds are available at SeedRenaissance.com. This is the hottest wild edible I have ever tasted. The heat is immediate and painful from leaves, flowers, and seed pods—so hot that my tongue felt slightly burned for days afterward. It is possible the heat may be dissipated by cooking, but I'm not going to test my theory to find out, just in case. Yikes! If you love hot, hot peppers, maybe this plant is for you! But the flowers put on a massive colorful show in late summer, and these are worth growing just for that alone.

63

Convolvulus arvensis

(FIELD BINDWEED)

U.S.: Found in all states except Alaska.

CANADA: Found everywhere except Newfoundland and Labrador, Northwest Territories, Nunavut, and Yukon.

EDIBLE PARTS: Leaves, flowers.

WHEN TO HARVEST: Summer, autumn.

FLOWER COLOR: White.

FORM: Slender twining vine.

HABITAT: Disturbed land, gardens, yards, fences, roadsides.

FLAVOR: Mild.

NOTES: The argument over whether the various species of bindweed are edible or not will probably never stop. Experts agree they have high levels of alkaloids in them, like rhubarb and many other plants, and everyone agrees that alkaloids can be difficult to remove from the body and can damage organ function over the long term. I've never had any problems with it, but this doesn't mean that it's not dangerous. There are many herbs and spices sold in the grocery store that are toxic at high levels and no one bats an eye at them because everyone just understands that cinnamon, for example, is something you only eat in small amounts. I eat field bindweed the same way—sparingly. Many people in the edible wild greens movement eat field bindweed, but many other people think we are crazy. In my experience, these people who think we who forage are crazy tend to drink soda, which is dangerously unhealthy, so there we are. If you are looking for an all-natural, even edible weed-killer recipe that kills invasions of this choking climber, visit SeedRensaissance.com.

Conyza canadensis

(HORSEWEED)

U.S.: Found in all states.

CANADA: Found everywhere except Newfoundland and Labrador, Nunavut, and Yukon.

EDIBLE PARTS: Leaves.

WHEN TO HARVEST: Spring, summer.

FLOWER COLOR: White.

FORM: Branched single-stem flower growing up to 3 feet tall.

HABITAT: Disturbed soil and waste spaces.

FLAVOR: Onion.

NOTES: A single-stem spiky plant becoming tall as it blooms. Seeds germinate in all but the coldest soils, and one plant can produce a quarter-million seeds—so we might as well start eating more of this aggressive weed. *Erigeron canadensis* is a synonym. This highly adaptable plant became resistant to glyphosate (Roundup) poison at the turn of the century, an example of how weeds fight back against humans. Horses can have reactions to touching or eating this plant, as do some humans. This plant is especially invasive in farm crops and has now spread from the U.S. to Europe.

Cornus Species

EDIBLE PARTS: Fruit.

WHEN TO HARVEST: Summer.

FLOWER COLOR: White.

FORM: Shrub.

HABITAT: Mountainsides, shady areas.

FLAVOR: Bitter.

NOTES: Dogwood berries are high in natural pectin, and you can use them to make pectin. However, they do not have a good flavor. One of my students once said the berries tasted like something you would use to clean your bathroom—astringent, bitter, and sour all at once. The petals of creeping dogwood form a striking square or diamond shape. Creeping dogwood does not grow in hot conditions. Western dogwood is widely sold as a landscape plant because of its bright red twigs and branches, which are most visible and sculptural in winter. We grow them in our yard for this purpose, and a winter drive through the canyons often reveals red dogwood lining the icy streams. Do not assume every species in the genus is edible. Never eat a wild edible unless you have specific information about the species first.

EDIBLE SPECIES EXAMPLES:

Cornus canadensis

> **U.S.:** Not found in United States.

> **CANADA:** Found in all provinces and territories.

Cornus sericea

> **U.S.:** Found in all states except Alabama, Arkansas, Florida, Georgia, Hawaii, Louisiana, Mississippi, Missouri, North Carolina, Oklahoma, South Carolina, Tennessee, and Texas.

> **CANADA:** Found in all provinces and territories.

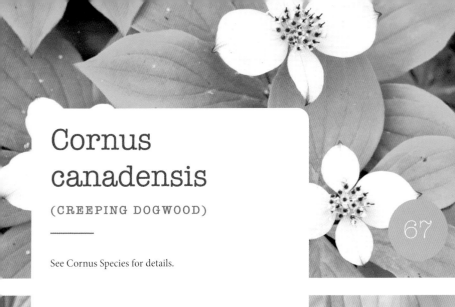

Cornus
canadensis

(CREEPING DOGWOOD)

————

See Cornus Species for details.

Cornus sericea

(WESTERN DOGWOOD)

See Cornus Species for details.

Corylus cornuta

(BEAKED HAZELNUT)

U.S.: Found in all states except Alaska, Arizona, Arkansas, Florida, Hawaii, Indiana, Kansas, Kentucky, Louisiana, Mississippi, Missouri, Nebraska, Nevada, New Mexico, Oklahoma, Texas, and Utah.

CANADA: Found everywhere except Newfoundland and Labrador, Northwest Territories, Nunavut, and Yukon.

EDIBLE PARTS: Nuts.

WHEN TO HARVEST: Autumn.

FLOWER COLOR: Yellow.

FORM: Shrubby deciduous thicket typically 4–8 feet tall, sometimes taller.

HABITAT: Mountainsides, shady areas.

FLAVOR: Nut.

NOTES: The name comes from the husk, which extends beyond the nut to form a beak. I live in the high mountain benches of the Rocky Mountains where these plants don't grow, but I planted one on the north side of my barn and it has happily thrived. I planted it because hazelnuts are great for you and have great flavor but are amazingly expensive to buy. Hazelnuts are a major ingredient in the beloved chocolate spread Nutella, and I already grow sweet stevia in my garden, so if I can just figure out how to grow a chocolate tree in the desert, maybe I can make my own sugar-free, stevia-sweetened chocolate spread.

Crataegus Species

U.S.: Found in all states except Hawaii.

CANADA: Found everywhere except Northwest Territory, Nunavut, and Yukon Territory.

EDIBLE PARTS: Fruit, flowers.

WHEN TO HARVEST: Autumn.

FLOWER COLOR: White.

FORM: Native tree.

HABITAT: Mountainsides.

FLAVOR: Mildly sweet. Some people describe the flavor as over-ripe apple.

NOTES: There are dozens of hawthorn species and all have edible berries. People use the berries to make jellies, sauces, and soups. Native American Indians commonly gathered the berry-sized fruits for eating fresh and drying as pressed cakes for winter use. Today, hawthorn berries, leaves, and flowers are used medicinally to help treat heart issues and can be found in all major pharmacy herb sections; they are probably one of the most widely used herbal medicines in North America. Hawthorns don't come by their name without reason. Depending on the species, they have thorns an inch or more long that can be straight or curved, so beware! To add insult to injury, some people have allergic reactions when punctured by these thorns. In the legend of Paul Bunyan, he uses the thorny hawthorn as a back scratcher. Hawthorns are also noted for their beautiful autumn leaf color display—they turn scarlet, orange, and purple. Birds and animals strongly favor the fruit and often clean up the whole tree, so there is little litter on the ground. Some experts say not to eat the seeds of hawthorn fruits, while others disagree.

EDIBLE SPECIES EXAMPLES:

Crataegus chrysocarpa

> **U.S.:** Found in all states except Alabama, Alaska, Arizona, Arkansas, California, Florida, Georgia, Hawaii, Kansas, Louisiana, Mississippi, Nevada, North Carolina, Oklahoma, South Carolina, Tennessee, and Texas.

> **CANADA:** Found everywhere except Newfoundland and Labrador, Northwest Territories, Nunavut, and Yukon.

Crataegus succulenta

> **U.S.:** Found in all states except Alabama, Alaska, California, Delaware, Hawaii, Louisiana, Maryland, Mississippi, Nevada, Oklahoma, South Carolina, and Texas.

> **CANADA:** Found everywhere except Newfoundland and Labrador, Northwest Territories, Nunavut, Saskatchewan, and Yukon.

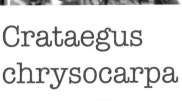

Crataegus chrysocarpa

(RED HAW TREE)

———

See Crataegus Species for details.

Crataegus succulenta

(FLESHY HAWTHORN)

See Crataegus Species for details.

Crepis Species

U.S.: Found in all states.

CANADA: Found in all provinces and territories.

EDIBLE PARTS: Leaves.

WHEN TO HARVEST: Spring.

FLOWER COLOR: Yellow.

FORM: Herbaceous flower typically growing about 12 inches tall.

HABITAT: Desert, strongly alkaline soi.l

FLAVOR: Mild.

NOTES: In early spring, when the plants have just emerged from the ground, *Crepis* species can look somewhat like salsify species, which emerges at the same time. Hawksbeards are more toothy at this stage than salsify, while salsify is more frilly, but both create an almost perfect circle of leaves low against the ground. Luckily, both salsify and hawksbeard are equally edible and delicious at this early stage, so even if you struggle to tell them apart, you can eat them. However, don't harvest the salsify leaves too much because then they won't form the parsnip-like root they are prized for. Do not assume every species in the genus is edible. Never eat a wild edible unless you have specific information about the species first.

EDIBLE SPECIES EXAMPLES:

Crepis capillaris

U.S.: Found in all states except Alabama, Arizona, Arkansas, Florida, Georgia, Louisiana, Minnesota, Mississippi, Nebraska, New Mexico, Oklahoma, South Carolina, South Dakota, and Wyoming.

CANADA: Found everywhere except Manitoba, Newfoundland and Labrador, Northwest Territories, Nunavut, Saskatchewan, and Yukon.

Crepis nana

U.S.: Not found in United States.

CANADA: Found in Alberta, British Columbia, Newfoundland and Labrador, Northwest Territories, Nunavut, and Yukon.

Crepis capillaris

(SMOOTH HAWKSBEARD)

See Crepis Species for details.

Crepis nana

(DWARF ALPINE HAWKBEARD)

———

See Crepis Species for details.

75

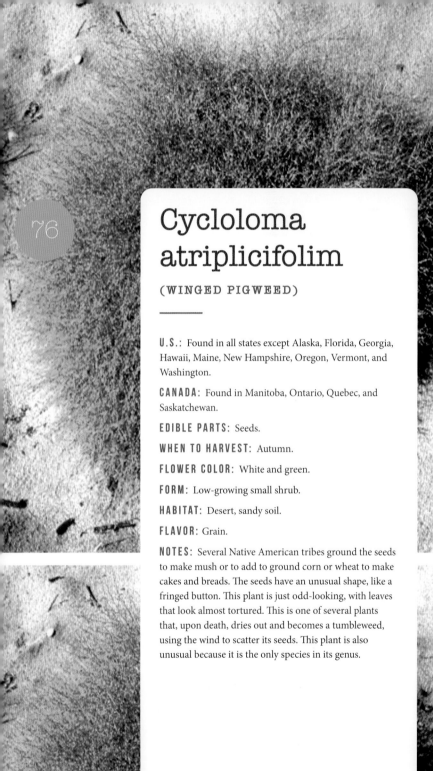

Cycloloma atriplicifolim

(WINGED PIGWEED)

———————

U.S.: Found in all states except Alaska, Florida, Georgia, Hawaii, Maine, New Hampshire, Oregon, Vermont, and Washington.

CANADA: Found in Manitoba, Ontario, Quebec, and Saskatchewan.

EDIBLE PARTS: Seeds.

WHEN TO HARVEST: Autumn.

FLOWER COLOR: White and green.

FORM: Low-growing small shrub.

HABITAT: Desert, sandy soil.

FLAVOR: Grain.

NOTES: Several Native American tribes ground the seeds to make mush or to add to ground corn or wheat to make cakes and breads. The seeds have an unusual shape, like a fringed button. This plant is just odd-looking, with leaves that look almost tortured. This is one of several plants that, upon death, dries out and becomes a tumbleweed, using the wind to scatter its seeds. This plant is also unusual because it is the only species in its genus.

Cynoglossum officinale

(HOUNDSTOUNGE, GYPSYFLOWER)

U.S.: Found in all states except Alaska, Florida, Hawaii, Louisiana, Mississippi, Oklahoma, and Texas.

CANADA: Found everywhere except Newfoundland and Labrador, Northwest Territories, Nunavut, and Yukon.

EDIBLE PARTS: Leaves (sparingly).

WHEN TO HARVEST: Summer.

FLOWER COLOR: Purple and red.

FORM: Biennial herbaceous flower growing up to four feet tall.

HABITAT: Clay soils in open, sunny spaces, wastelands, roadsides.

FLAVOR: Bitter.

NOTES: Leaves are used, fresh or dry, to protect stored veggies from animals and to protect gardens from moles, mice, rats, and other critters. This plant is also grown around homes to provide the same natural pest repellent properties. Historically the leaves have been eaten, but today we know they are high in alkaloids, and even reportedly somewhat narcotic when eaten in large quantities. Some reports even say the plant many be carcinogenic. This plant is also strongly medicinal and has been used medicinally for many years. My friends and I gather it in late spring for medicinal purposes. The flavor is not good, so perhaps it is best to leave this to be a medicinal and pest control plant. The seeds are covered in velcro-like hairs that are difficult to get out of clothes, socks, shoes, and pet hair.

Cyperus Species

EDIBLE PARTS: Leaves, nut-like tuber, seeds.

WHEN TO HARVEST: Summer, autumn.

FLOWER COLOR: Green.

FORM: Low-growing grass with seed tufts.

HABITAT: Open, sunny disturbed land, roadsides, wastelands.

FLAVOR: Seeds have a grain flavor, tubers have a more nutty flavor. Leaves are mild in spring.

NOTES: There are hundreds of species in this genus, and dozens may be subspecies instead of true species. It is likely no one knows how many of these species are edible. The Pennsylvania Germans used to make a marzipan-type candy by pounding the sedge nuts with sugar.

EDIBLE SPECIES EXAMPLES:

Cyperus erythrorhizos

> **U.S.:** Found in all states except Alaska, Hawaii, and Vermont.

> **CANADA:** Found in British Columbia, Manitoba, and Ontario.

Cyperus esculentus

> **U.S.:** Found in all states except Alaska, Montana, and Wyoming.

> **CANADA:** Found in British Columbia, New Brunswick, Nova Scotia, Ontario, Prince Edward Island, and Quebec.

Cyperus odoratus

> **U.S.:** Found in all states except Alaska, Montana, Nevada, Utah, and Wyoming.

> **CANADA:** Found in Ontario and Quebec.

Cyperus schweinitzii

> **U.S.:** Found in all states except Alabama, Alaska, California, Connecticut, Delaware, Florida, Georgia, Hawaii, Louisiana, Maine, Maryland, Mississippi, Nevada, New Hampshire, North Carolina, Rhode Island, South Carolina, Tennessee, Vermont, Virginia, and West Virginia.

> **CANADA:** Found in Alberta, Manitoba, New Brunswick, Nova Scotia, Ontario, Prince Edward Island, Quebec, and Saskatchewan.

Cyperus squarrosus

> **U.S.:** Found in all states except Alaska and Hawaii.

> **CANADA:** Found in Alberta, British Columbia, Manitoba, New Brunswick, Ontario, Quebec, and Saskatchewan.

Cyperus erythrorhizos

(REDROOT FLATSEDGE)

See Cyperus Species for details.

Cyperus esculentus

(YELLOW NUTSEDGE)

———————

See Cyperus Species for details.

Cyperus odoratus

(FRAGRANT FLATSEDGE)

See Cyperus Species for details.

Cyperus schweinitzii

(SCHWEINITZ'S FLATSEDGE)

———

See Cyperus Species for details.

Cyperus squarrosus

(BEARDED FLATSEDGE)

See Cyperus Species for details.

Daucus carota

(WILD CARROT)

U.S.: Found in all states except Alaska and Hawaii

CANADA: Found everywhere except Alberta, Northwest Territories, Nunavut, and Yukon.

EDIBLE PARTS: Root, flowerheads (cooked), seeds (used as spice).

WHEN TO HARVEST: Summer.

FLOWER COLOR: White.

FORM: Slender flower typically growing four feet tall.

HABITAT: Open sunny spaces, fields, roadsides, wastelands, gardens, fence-lines.

FLAVOR: Carrot.

NOTES: All modern domesticated carrots come from this genus, and when you pull these weeds by the root, the smell of carrots is unmistakable. This plant is widely used medicinally. This plant is not native to North America, having come over from Europe, but it has sure made itself at home. It provides nectar for bees, wasps, flies, and beetles. The seeds provide food for pheasants, grouse, and mice. On my property, these plants like to vex me by growing right up in the fences, making it almost impossible to clean these out of the fenceline. The roots taste best and are most tender before this plant bolts to flower; during and after flowering they can be fibrous to the point of being unchewable.

Descurainia Species

EDIBLE PARTS: Leaves, seeds.

WHEN TO HARVEST: Spring, summer.

FLOWER COLOR: Yellow.

FORM: Slender, multi-stemmed flower typically growing about twelve inches tall.

HABITAT: Disturbed spaces, wastelands, pastures, fields, roadsides, mountainsides.

NOTES: Leaves are bitter. Seeds have a mustardy grain flavor. Native Americans widely used the seeds in porridges, cakes, breads, and more. Flixweed seeds are twenty-five percent protein. This plant produces a lot of seeds. Flixweed seems to grow everywhere in the West and is not picky about soil or conditions. The life cycle of this plant is short and it is usually dead by the heat of summer. The pronounced seed pods are very typical of the mustard family.

EDIBLE SPECIES EXAMPLES:

Descurainia pinnata

> **U.S.:** Found in all states except Alabama, Alaska, and Hawaii.
>
> **CANADA:** Found everywhere except New Brunswick, Newfoundland and Labrador, and Nunavut.

Descurinia sophia

> **U.S.:** Found in all states except Alabama and Florida.
>
> **CANADA:** Found everywhere except Newfoundland and Labrador and Nunavut.

86

Descurainia pinnata

(PENNSYLVANIA BITTERCRESS)

See Descurainia Species for details.

Descurainia sophia

(FLIXWEED, HERB SOPHIA)

———

See Descurainia Species for details.

87

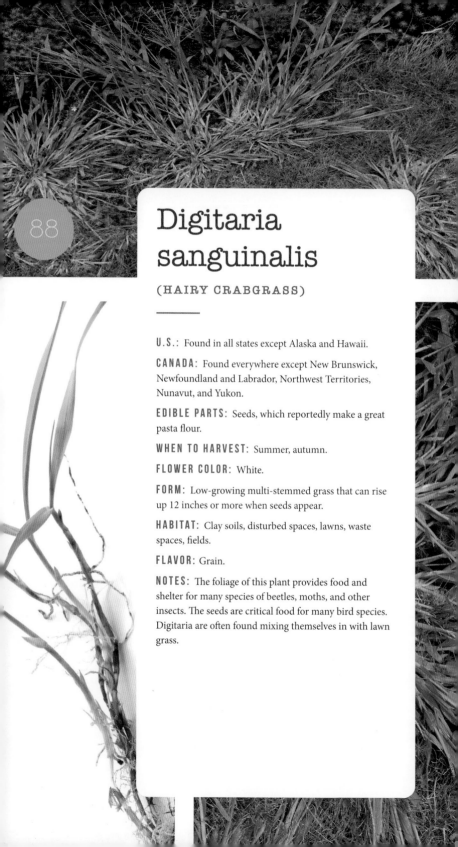

Digitaria sanguinalis

(HAIRY CRABGRASS)

U.S.: Found in all states except Alaska and Hawaii.

CANADA: Found everywhere except New Brunswick, Newfoundland and Labrador, Northwest Territories, Nunavut, and Yukon.

EDIBLE PARTS: Seeds, which reportedly make a great pasta flour.

WHEN TO HARVEST: Summer, autumn.

FLOWER COLOR: White.

FORM: Low-growing multi-stemmed grass that can rise up 12 inches or more when seeds appear.

HABITAT: Clay soils, disturbed spaces, lawns, waste spaces, fields.

FLAVOR: Grain.

NOTES: The foliage of this plant provides food and shelter for many species of beetles, moths, and other insects. The seeds are critical food for many bird species. Digitaria are often found mixing themselves in with lawn grass.

Elaeagnus Species

EDIBLE PARTS: Fruit, seed.

WHEN TO HARVEST: Summer.

FLOWER COLOR: Yellow.

FORM: Tree growing to thirty-five feet tall.

HABITAT: Usually found near streams, marshes, and other natural water sources.

FLAVOR: Slightly sweet, but only when fully ripe.

NOTES: One way to tell these two species apart is that Russian olives have thorns and silverberries do not. Both fix nitrogen in the soil. These non-native trees were originally brought to desert areas because they grow so fast, providing firewood, shade, and food. These trees are often considered "trash" trees because they spread easily, grow rapidly, and withstand drought easily. They are not easy to get rid of.

EDIBLE SPECIES EXAMPLES:

Elaeangus angustifolia

> **U.S.:** Found in all states except Alabama, Alaska, Arkansas, Florida, Georgia, Hawaii, Indiana, Louisiana, Mississippi, New Hampshire, South Carolina, and West Virginia.

> **CANADA:** Found everywhere except Newfoundland and Labrador, Northwest Territories, Nunavut, and Yukon.

Elaeangus commutata

> **U.S.:** Not found in United States.

> **CANADA:** Found everywhere except New Brunswick, Newfoundland and Labrador, Nova Scotia, and Prince Edward Island.

90

Elaeagnus angustifolia

(RUSSIAN OLIVE)

———

See Elaeangus Species for details.

Elaeagnus commutata

(SILVERBERRY)

————

See Elaeangus Species for details.

Eleusine indica

(GOOSEGRASS)

U.S.: Found in all states except Alaska, Idaho, Montana, Washington, and Wyoming.

CANADA: Found in Ontario and Quebec.

EDIBLE PARTS: Seeds, leaves, roots.

WHEN TO HARVEST: Spring, summer.

FLOWER COLOR: Green.

FORM: Low-growing grass rising up twelve to eighteen inches when bearing seeds.

HABITAT: Wastelands, roadsides, lawns, disturbed areas.

FLAVOR: Seeds have a grain flavor. Leaves can be mild but fibrous. Roots are less useful because they are small and hard to clean. This species looks similar to *Digitaria* species. Some insects use the plant for food, but birds don't seem to like it much. Goosegrass is common in sidewalk cracks.

Elymus repens

(QUACKGRASS)

U.S.: Found in all states except Alabama, Florida, Georgia, Hawaii, Louisiana, and South Carolina.

CANADA: Found in all provinces and territories.

EDIBLE PARTS: Leaves.

WHEN TO HARVEST: Spring, summer.

FLOWER COLOR: Green.

FORM: Grass growing up to three feet tall.

HABITAT: Pastures, lawns, fields, gardens, roadsides, waste spaces.

FLAVOR: Grassy and fibrous.

NOTES: This horrible non-native plant is an environmental disaster that has caused so much damage, including to my own property. To think that someone actually brought this plant to the U.S. inspires thoughts of revenge. We should find this historical person and make them come back and clean up their mess! This plant is the bane of many gardeners because it spreads by rhizome beneath the ground and cannot be killed by any weedkiller (it can be temporarily knocked back, but because it spreads underground, it just grows back in). I'm fond of telling people that this plant may have been created by Lucifer himself. This plant was likely brought to the U.S. by settlers for use as a pasture grass, but today it invades and destroys gardens, flower beds, and gravel driveways by choking out everything. If you can't tell already, I hate this plant. Today the seeds of quackgrass are still sometimes sold in pasture grass mixes, and selling the seeds should be illegal.

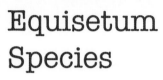

Equisetum Species

EDIBLE PARTS: Tubers, newly emerged stems (cooked only) (small quantities only).

WHEN TO HARVEST: Spring, summer, autumn.

FLOWER COLOR: The flower has a very striking and unusual pagoda-like shape and is green and black. In spring the plant looks like spears, and in summer it is almost thickly feathery. Overall the plant looks and acts like something created by Dr. Seuss.

FORM: Single-stem grass that resembles a dart in spring and a horse's tail in summer when its needle-like leaves are out.

HABITAT: Grows in water or wet soil.

FLAVOR: Grassy asparagus-like.

NOTES: This is one of those rare plants that was heavily eaten historically but probably should never be eaten today. Why? Because test after test has shown that *Equisetum* is fantastic at pulling heavy metals out of the soil. Two hundred years ago this was probably not an issue, but today, air pollution, mining debris, car exhaust, and many other sources lace our soil and water with heavy metals no matter where we live. So instead of eating this plant, we should probably all grow it in our gardens and harvest it and throw it away, allowing it to clean the soil and take the toxins to the landfill. This plant should not be composted, because then the heavy metals go right back into the ground. Also, while we actually probably should grow this in our gardens, note that it takes a lot of water and is invasive and hard to eradicate. In addition, while this plant has a long history as an edible wild food, modern studies have shown it contains an enzyme that can destroy vitamin B in the body when eaten in large amounts. I use this plant in my homemade toothpaste recipe, which you can find in my book *More Forgotten Skills of Self-Sufficiency*. However, my friends and I have been careful to find places to harvest this plant where we feel certain it is free from heavy metal contamination—finding such a spot requires some hiking. We harvest this plant each year to try and use medicinally and for toothpaste.

EDIBLE SPECIES EXAMPLES:

Equisetum arvense

U.S.: Found in all states except Florida, Hawaii, and Louisiana.

CANADA: Found in all provinces and territories.

Equisetum laevigatum

U.S.: Found in all states except Alabama, Alaska, Delaware, Florida, Georgia, Hawaii, Louisiana, Maine, Maryland, Massachusetts, Mississippi, New Hampshire, New Jersey, North Carolina, Rhode Island, South Carolina, Tennessee, Vermont, Virginia, and West Virginia.

CANADA: Found in Alberta, British Columbia, Manitoba, Ontario, Quebec, and Saskatchewan.

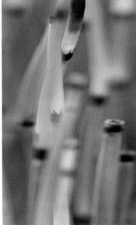

Equisetum hyemale

U.S.: Found in all states except Hawaii.

CANADA: Found everywhere except Newfoundland and Labrador and Nunavut.

Equisetum pratense

U.S.: Not found in United States.

CANADA: Found in all provinces and territories.

Equisetum scirpoides

U.S.: Not found in United States.

CANADA: Found in all provinces and territories.

Equisetum variegatum

U.S.: Not found in United States

CANADA: Found in all provinces and territories.

Equisetum arvense

(HORSETAIL GRASS)

See Equisetum Species for details.

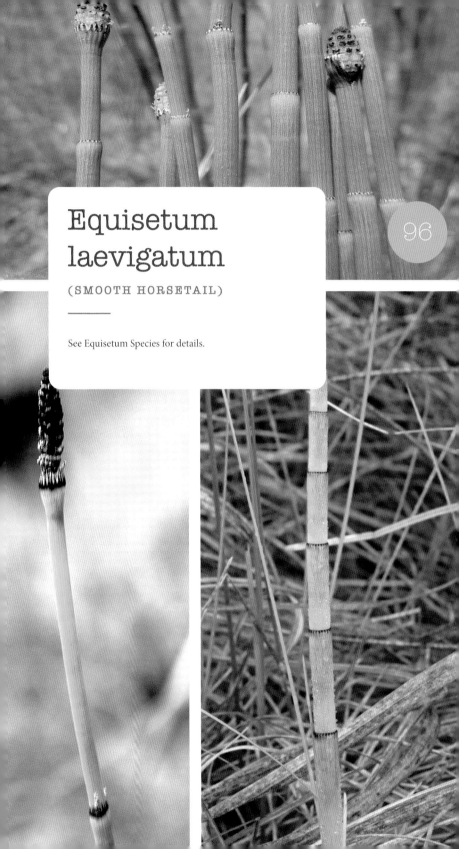

Equisetum laevigatum

(SMOOTH HORSETAIL)

———

See Equisetum Species for details.

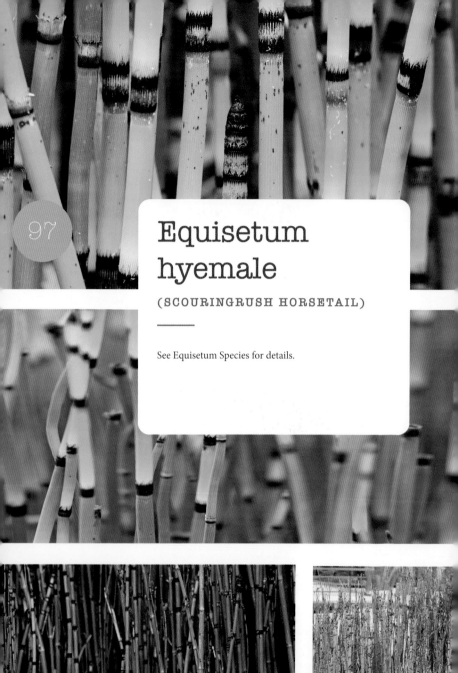

Equisetum hyemale

(SCOURINGRUSH HORSETAIL)

———

See Equisetum Species for details.

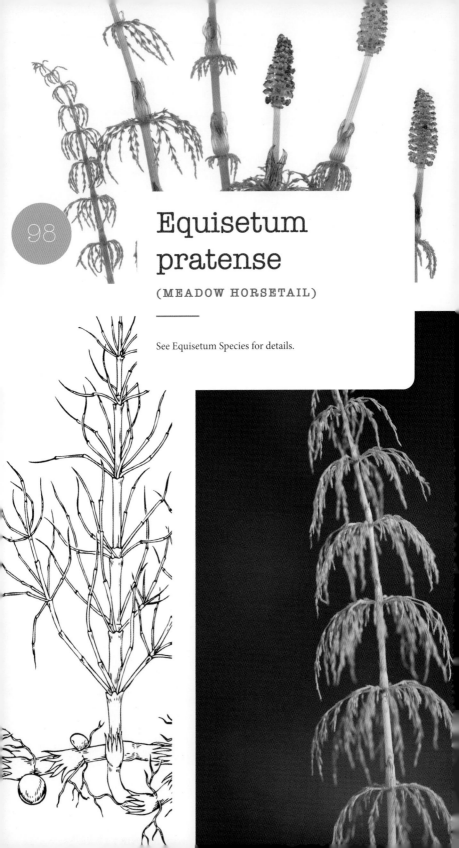

Equisetum pratense

(MEADOW HORSETAIL)

See Equisetum Species for details.

Equisetum scirpoides

(DWARF SCOURINGRUSH)

————

See Equisetum Species for details.

Equisetum variegatum

(VARIEGATED SCOURINGRUSH)

———

See Equisetum Species for details.

100

Erodium cicutarium

(REDSTEM FILAREE, STORK'S BILL)

U.S.: Found in all states except Florida.

CANADA: Found everywhere except Newfoundland and Labrador, Northwest Territories, Nunavut, and Yukon.

EDIBLE PARTS: Leaves, flowers, roots, stems.

WHEN TO HARVEST: Spring.

FLOWER COLOR: Light purple.

FORM: Small annual flower typically growing about six inches tall.

HABITAT: Disturbed land, pastures, fields.

FLAVOR: Mild. Leaves taste best before the flower emerges. This plant gets its name from the seed pods, which resemble a stork's bill. It is often found close to the ground in a beautiful mass of flowers in spring. *"Erodium"* is Greek for "heron," noting the seed pods' resemblance to a stork or heron bill. One botanical expert says the Navajo used this plant medicinally—get this—to treat bobcat and mountain lion bites. If that little factoid doesn't make you appreciate how our lives are different from the generations that came before us, nothing will. Just try to picture someone gathering this plant for that purpose. It's hard to imagine that kind of life, thank goodness.

Fragaria Species

EDIBLE PARTS: Berries, leaves.

WHEN TO HARVEST: Summer, autumn.

FLOWER COLOR: White.

FORM: Small multi-stemmed flower.

HABITAT: Mountainsides and forests in dappled light or shade.

FLAVOR: The berries are a burst of sweetness that beats anything found in stores. The leaves are mild.

NOTES: Probably billions of wild strawberry plants grow in the Rocky Mountains, taking advantage of the cooler temperatures and relatively high humidity in the forests at elevation. The berries rarely get larger than a pea because these plants often grown in shade, but sometimes you get lucky. Finding ripe strawberries can be a real challenge because many creatures of the woods, large and small, also find these berries delicious and begin eating them even before they turn red and ripe. Competition is fierce for the ripe berries, so whenever my wife and I find one, it makes our hike extra special. Ripening times can vary widely, depending on elevation, weather patterns, shade, soil alkalinity or acidity, and more. I teach classes where I take groups into forests, deserts, and suburban pockets to help people identify the best wild berries and where to find them in places they can be legally harvested. You can find information about my various classes, sign up for my newsletter, or buy seeds for native strawberries at SeedRenaissance.com (signups in the bottom left corner of the website homepage).

EDIBLE SPECIES EXAMPLES:

Fragaria vesca

U.S.: Found in all states except Alabama, Alaska, Arkansas, Florida, Georgia, Kansas, Louisiana, Mississippi, Nevada, Oklahoma, and South Carolina.

CANADA: Found everywhere except Newfoundland and Labrador, Nunavut, and Yukon.

Fragaria virginiana

U.S.: Found in all states except Hawaii.

CANADA: Found in all provinces and territories.

Fragaria vesca

(WOODLAND, ALPINE, OR WILD STRAWBERRY)

———————

See Fragaria Species for details.

103

Fragaria virginiana

(VIRGINIA STRAWBERRY)

———

See Fragaria Species for details.

Galium aparine

(CLEAVERS, GOOSEGRASS)

U.S.: Found in all states except Hawaii.

CANADA: Found everywhere except Newfoundland and Labrador, Northwest Territories, Nunavut, and Yukon.

EDIBLE PARTS: Young leaves.

WHEN TO HARVEST: Spring.

FLOWER COLOR: White.

FORM: Herbaceous annual growing less than a foot tall.

HABITAT: Mountainsides.

FLAVOR: Fresh and mild.

NOTES: Cleavers can be easy to miss when hiking or foraging because it has spindly, thin stalks and often grows among native grasses, but once you know what it looks like, you will find it many places growing in spring shade. The leaves can be hard to chew and are easiest to eat cooked, but I always just eat them raw anyway. They are used medicinally to help lymph movement and so I grow them in my garden and dry them for year-round use too. My friends and I gather armloads of this plant from the mountains for medical use. For many centuries the stems of this sticky plant have been woven together and dried for use as a sieve. This plant is also known by dozens of regional names. This plant is also well known to children because the soft edible barbs stick easily to clothing, making them a fun, free throwing toy. This trait is how the plant got it name—"apairo" (*aparine*) in Greek means "seize" or "grab" because this plant does this so well. Rarely people reportedly get a rash from touching this sticky plant. I don't know anyone this has happened to, but if the plants irritates you, common sense says don't eat it.

Gaultheria hispidula

(CREEPING SNOWBERRY)

U.S.: Not found in United States.

CANADA: Found everywhere except Northwest Territories and Yukon.

EDIBLE PARTS: Leaves and berries.

WHEN TO HARVEST: Summer, Autumn.

FLOWER COLOR: White.

FORM: Low-growing shrub.

HABITAT: Moist mountain areas with shade and humidity.

FLAVOR: Wintergreen.

NOTES: These plants are cousins of *G. procumbens,* which is the plant that is widely used to produce wintergreen oil that flavors so many products that people love for their revitalizing and medically useful fragrance. I love what the U.S. Forest Service website says about these plants: "The berries are edible and have a spectacular wintergreen flavor, similar to the related wintergreen plant (*Gaultheria procumbens*). The flavor is more concentrated in the snowberry, and has been compared with that of a wet Tic-Tac." So next time you are foraging in the mountains with friends, I dare you to ask "Would anyone like a wet Tic-Tac-like berry?"

Geranium bicknellii

(BICKNELL'S CRANESBILL)

――――――

U.S.: Found in all states except Alabama, Arizona, Arkansas, Delaware, Florida, Georgia, Hawaii, Kansas, Kentucky, Louisiana, Maryland, Mississippi, Nebraska, Nevada, New Mexico, North Carolina, Oklahoma, South Carolina, and Texas.

CANADA: Found everywhere except Newfoundland and Labrador and Nunavut.

EDIBLE PARTS: Flowers, leaves.

WHEN TO HARVEST: Spring.

FLOWER COLOR: Pink/Light purple or white.

FORM: Perennial flower typically growing up to three feet tall.

HABITAT: Shady or dappled mountainsides.

FLAVOR: Mild.

NOTES: The leaves can be sticky and hairy and don't have a texture that makes you want to eat them, even though they are edible. The flower petals are the best part of these plants for eating. There are many species of wild geraniums and some are hard to tell apart and no one knows if all of them are edible. The flowers of this species are beautiful.

Helianthus Species

EDIBLE PARTS: Seeds raw, roasted, or sprouted. Immature flower buds fresh or steamed. Oil from seeds. Tubers of some perennials species, including *H. tuberosus*, *H. cusickii*, and others.

WHEN TO HARVEST: Summer.

FLOWER COLOR: Yellow.

FORM: Single-stem tall flower.

HABITAT: Roadsides, disturbed lands, desert lands.

FLAVOR: The seeds are nutty, the buds are mild and slightly sweet and resinous.

NOTES: The seeds are easiest to harvest and eat at the moment the petals begin to wilt off the flowerhead because the hull is soft and can simply be eaten with the nut inside, no shelling necessary. If you wait until the hull begins to harden, removing the hulls can be difficult. I suggest putting the dried sunflower seeds in a blender and pulsing slightly to crack the hulls, or pound the hulls, and then winnow to separate the seed pieces from hulls. However, this method can still leave little pieces of hull if not done carefully. *H. tuberosus* (sunchokes) is widely grown in self-reliance gardens and backyard food forests, including mine, because it is a variety of sunflower that produces a potato-like root that is excellent when boiled or baked and actually far healthier than common potatoes because it does not spike the glycemic load when eaten.

EDIBLE SPECIES EXAMPLES:

Helianthus annus

   U.S.: Found in all states.

   CANADA: Found everywhere except Newfoundland
and Labrador, Nunavut, and Yukon.

Helianthus maximiliani

   U.S.: Found in all states except Alaska, Arizona,
Florida, Georgia, Hawaii, Louisiana, Nevada, New
Hampshire, Oregon, Utah, and Vermont.

   CANADA: Found in Alberta, British Columbia,
Manitoba, Ontario, Quebec, and Saskatchewan.

Helianthus pauciflorus

   U.S.: Found in all states except Alabama,
Alaska, California, Florida, Hawaii, Idaho, Louisiana,
Nevada, North Carolina, Ohio, Oregon, South Carolina,
Tennessee, Utah, Washington, and West Virginia.

   CANADA: Found everywhere except
Newfoundland and Labrador, Northwest
Territories, and Nunavut.

Helianthus petiolaris

   U.S.: Found in all states except Alabama,
Alaska, Florida, Georgia, Hawaii,
Kentucky, Mississippi, and New Hampshire.

   CANADA: Found in Alberta, Manitoba,
Ontario, and Saskatchewan.

Helianthus tuberosus

   U.S.: Found in all states except Alaska,
Arizona, Hawaii, Nevada, and New Mexico.

   CANADA: Found in Manitoba, New
Brunswick, Nova Scotia, Ontario,
Prince Edward Island, Quebec, and Saskatchewan.

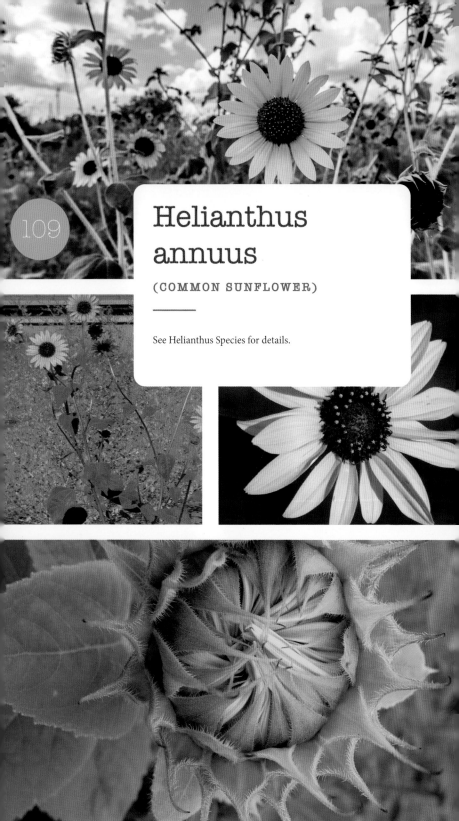

Helianthus annuus

(COMMON SUNFLOWER)

———

See Helianthus Species for details.

Helianthus maximiliani

(MAXIMILIAN SUNFLOWER)

See Helianthus Species for details.

Helianthus pauciflorus

(STIFF SUNFLOWER)

See Helianthus Species for details.

Helianthus petiolaris

(PRAIRIE SUNFLOWER)

See Helianthus Species for details.

Helianthus tuberosus

(SUNCHOKES, JERUSALEM ARTICHOKE)

————

See Helianthus Species for details.

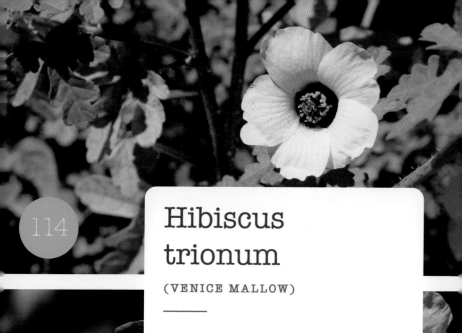

Hibiscus trionum

(VENICE MALLOW)

U.S.: Found in all states except Alabama, Alaska, Hawaii, and Nevada.

CANADA: Found in Manitoba, New Brunswick, Nova Scotia, Ontario, Prince Edward Island, Quebec, and Saskatchewan.

EDIBLE PARTS: Leaves.

WHEN TO HARVEST: Spring, autumn, rarely summer.

FLOWER COLOR: White petals with a purple base.

FORM: Branching flower typically growing 18 inches tall.

HABITAT: Gardens, pasture, disturbed land.

FLAVOR: Mild radishy.

NOTES: This plant has an unusually large and showy flower for its size, and a century ago it was grown as a landscaping plant for its beauty. For some reason, the leaves of this plant always look to me like they should be delicious, but they are not that great because they are chewy and hard to swallow. The flowers look like groundcherry pods before they open. These have planted themselves in my winter greenhouses and I just leave them alone because I like the flowers.

Hordeum jubatum

(FOXTAIL BARELY, SQUIRREL-TAIL GRASS)

———

U.S.: Found in all states except Alabama, Florida, Georgia, Hawaii, Louisiana, and Mississippi.

CANADA: Found in all provinces and territories.

EDIBLE PARTS: Seeds raw, roasted, or ground for flour.

WHEN TO HARVEST: Summer, autumn.

FLOWER COLOR: Green.

FORM: Single-stem grass typically growing 18 inches tall.

HABITAT: Fields, pastures, meadows, wastelands.

FLAVOR: Grain.

NOTES: This grass often forms colonies when it finds a sunny location that it likes. The seeds are sold by some companies as a landscaping ornamental because of the graceful way the grain moves in a breeze, and because landscaping grasses have been popular in recent years.

Juglans nigra

(BLACK WALNUT)

U.S.: Found in all states except Alaska, Arizona, California, Hawaii, Idaho, Montana, Nevada, Oregon, Washington, and Wyoming.

CANADA: Found in Manitoba, Ontario, and Quebec.

EDIBLE PARTS: Nuts.

WHEN TO HARVEST: Autumn.

FLOWER COLOR: Pink.

FORM: Tree.

HABITAT: Sunny spaces near water.

FLAVOR: Nut.

NOTES: All Juglans species can be tapped for sweet-tasting syrup according to AmericanForests.org. It should be noted that there is a lot of misinformation circulating about how black walnuts can kill vegetable gardens and that the wood and leaves shouldn't be used for mulch or compost, but the Extension Service says the truth is that only a few plants are actually affected by black walnut. In medicinal herb circles, the tinctured green immature hulls of black walnuts are famous for treating some species of fungal infections. The hulls are also used to make black or dark brown dye, and the medicinal tincture itself can be staining. The tincture is widely sold in health food stores and online. If you are new to the world of herbal medicine, my book *Forgotten Skills of Backyard Herbal Healing and Family Health* is a great place to start. Find it at Amazon.com.

Kochia scoparia

(KOCHIA)

U.S.: Found in all states except Alabama, Alaska, Arkansas, Florida, Georgia, Hawaii, and Maryland.

CANADA: Found in Alberta, British Columbia, Manitoba, New Brunswick, Ontario, Quebec, and Saskatchewan.

EDIBLE PARTS: Leaves and seeds.

WHEN TO HARVEST: Summer.

FLOWER COLOR: Green.

FORM: Pyramid-shaped herb growing up to five feet tall.

HABITAT: Desert, waste spaces, roadsides, ditch banks, disturbed soil.

FLAVOR: Mild.

NOTES: Seeds are twenty percent protein and eight percent fat. The pollen is a common allergen. If you suffer from allergies, see the section in this book on stinging nettle. I am violently allergic to kochia pollen, but nettle has resolved this for me and I only wish I had known about nettle and allergies years earlier. Perhaps part of the reason so many people are allergic to this plant is because it is allelopathic, meaning it is part of a special class of botanicals that produce their own natural herbicides to kill their neighboring plants. This allows kochia to form dense stands—little kochia forests.

Lactuca pulchella

(BLUE LETTUCE)

———

U.S.: Found in all states except Arkansas, Connecticut, Delaware, Florida, Georgia, Hawaii, Kentucky, Maryland, Massachusetts, Mississippi, New Hampshire, North Carolina, Rhode Island, South Carolina, Tennessee, Vermont, Virginia, and West Virginia.

CANADA: Found everywhere except New Brunswick, Newfoundland and Labrador, Nova Scotia, Nunavut, Prince Edward Island, and Yukon.

EDIBLE PARTS: Young leaves.

WHEN TO HARVEST: Spring, summer.

FLOWER COLOR: Blue.

FORM: Single-stem flower typically growing up to two feet tall.

HABITAT: Roadsides, waste spaces, disturbed soil.

FLAVOR: Mild.

NOTES: This plant has a long history of medicinal use. *Mulgedium pulchellum* and *L. tatarica var. Pulchella* are synonyms. The flowers can be confused with chicory. Experts disagree about whether it is a perennial or biennial.

Lamium Species

EDIBLE PARTS: Leaves, flowers.

WHEN TO HARVEST: Spring.

FLOWER COLOR: Red, purple.

FORM: Low-growing herb unusual for its upright flowers above the foliage.

HABITAT: Waste spaces, gardens.

FLAVOR: Herbaceous, ranging from mild to grassy to radishy.

NOTES: These cousins are both members of the mint family. They have some resemblance to nettle leaves, but they have no sting. Every time I teach students about purple dead nettle (also called red dead nettle), I get the same response: no one wants to eat something with the word "dead" in the name. *Lamium* is from the Greek word for "throat," and *purpureum* means purple, so the Latin name refers to the purple trumpet flowers. I have never been able to find an explanation for the reason why dead is in the name, or for this plant's other name, purple archangel. My only guess about the reason for these names comes from a great two-book set published in 1931 and still in print today (and worth owning) called A Modern Herbal by Mrs. M. Grieve, which says that purple dead nettle has been used for centuries to stop bleeding in wounds. This could explain the "dead" reference in the name, and also the reference to "archangel." I have never tried using the leaves to stop bleeding and I have no idea if it works, but I know there are other herbs that do stop bleeding, so I don't doubt the veracity of the claim. It is also possible that "dead" refers to the highly unusual habit this plant has of the leaves turning purple on top as it matures, giving the (incorrect) appearance that the plant is dying from the top down. At any rate, I've eaten these a lot, and both plants are widely eaten by foragers like me all over the country, so there is no question of their safety.

EDIBLE SPECIES EXAMPLES:

Lamium amplexicaule

> **U.S.:** Found in all states except Alaska.

> **CANADA:** Found everywhere except Nunavut and Yukon.

Lamium purpureum

> **U.S.:** Found in all states except Arizona, Hawaii, Minnesota, Nevada, New Mexico, North Dakota, South Dakota, and Wyoming.

> **CANADA:** Found in British Columbia, Newfoundland and Labrador, New Brunswick, Nova Scotia, Ontario, Prince Edward Island, and Quebec.

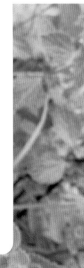

Lamium amplexicaule

(HENBIT)

———

See Lamium Species for details.

Lamium purpureum

(PURPLE DEAD NETTLE)

———

See Lamium Species for details.

121

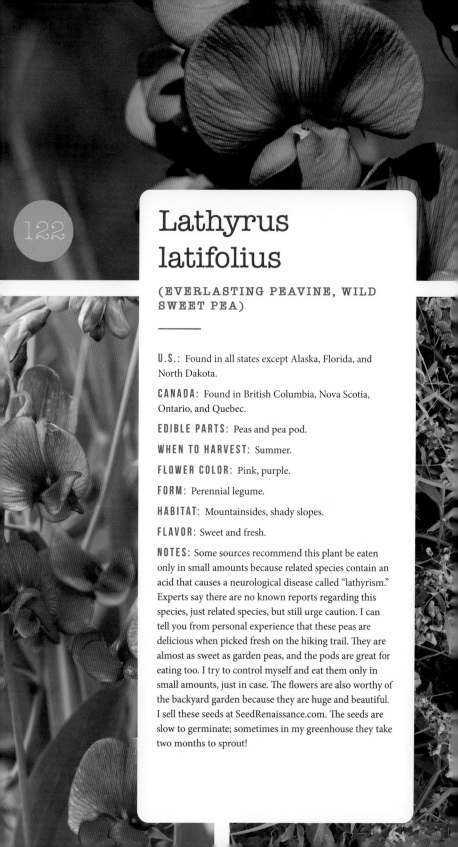

Lathyrus latifolius

(EVERLASTING PEAVINE, WILD SWEET PEA)

U.S.: Found in all states except Alaska, Florida, and North Dakota.

CANADA: Found in British Columbia, Nova Scotia, Ontario, and Quebec.

EDIBLE PARTS: Peas and pea pod.

WHEN TO HARVEST: Summer.

FLOWER COLOR: Pink, purple.

FORM: Perennial legume.

HABITAT: Mountainsides, shady slopes.

FLAVOR: Sweet and fresh.

NOTES: Some sources recommend this plant be eaten only in small amounts because related species contain an acid that causes a neurological disease called "lathyrism." Experts say there are no known reports regarding this species, just related species, but still urge caution. I can tell you from personal experience that these peas are delicious when picked fresh on the hiking trail. They are almost as sweet as garden peas, and the pods are great for eating too. I try to control myself and eat them only in small amounts, just in case. The flowers are also worthy of the backyard garden because they are huge and beautiful. I sell these seeds at SeedRenaissance.com. The seeds are slow to germinate; sometimes in my greenhouse they take two months to sprout!

Lepidium perfoliatum

(CLASPING PEPPERWEED)

U.S.: Found in all states except Alabama, Florida, Hawaii, Indiana, Louisiana, New Hampshire, New Jersey, and Vermont.

CANADA: Found everywhere except Manitoba, New Brunswick, Newfoundland and Labrador, Northwest Territories, Nova Scotia, Nunavut, Prince Edward Island, and Yukon.

EDIBLE PARTS: Leaves of both species, root of L. latifolium.

WHEN TO HARVEST: Spring.

FLOWER COLOR: White.

FORM: Small single-stemmed branching herb known for its shield-like leaves.

HABITAT: Gardens, disturbed soil, roadsides.

FLAVOR: Horseradish.

NOTES: If you like horseradish, you will love this plant. My students either love it or hate it because the flavor is strong and immediate. It's called pepperweed for a reason. *Perfoliatum* is Latin for "with the leaf surrounding the stem," which refers to the unusual way the leaf wraps itself on the plant.

Lolium perenne

(ITALIAN RYEGRASS)

U.S.: Found in all states.

CANADA: Found everywhere except Newfoundland and Labrador and Nunavut.

EDIBLE PARTS: Seeds.

WHEN TO HARVEST: Summer, autumn.

FLOWER COLOR: Green.

FORM: Perennial multi-stem grass.

HABITAT: Disturbed land, roadsides, pastures, waste spaces.

FLAVOR: Grain.

NOTES: Since the 1960s, this grass has been sold and cultivated as lawn turf because it is perennial and withstands mowing well. Today there are dozens of cultivars sold for this purpose. Some experts say this was likely the first pasture grass ever planted specifically for that purpose by settlers. It has been cultivated for pasture and lawn use in England for three centuries and was brought to North America by settlers.

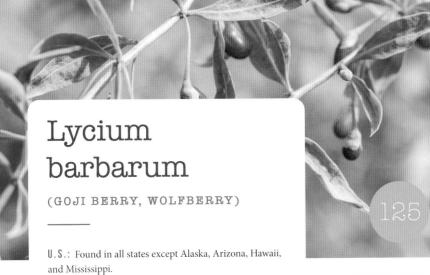

Lycium barbarum

(GOJI BERRY, WOLFBERRY)

———

U.S.: Found in all states except Alaska, Arizona, Hawaii, and Mississippi.

CANADA: Found everywhere except Manitoba, New Brunswick, Newfoundland and Labrador, Northwest Territories, Nunavut, Prince Edward Island, and Yukon.

EDIBLE PARTS: Berries.

WHEN TO HARVEST: Spring, late summer.

FLOWER COLOR: Purple.

FORM: Woody perennial.

HABITAT: Moist, open, sunny soil ranging from deserts to mountains.

FLAVOR: Sweet.

NOTES: These plants produce two berry crops a year, one in spring and one in early autumn. Occasionally a third crop is possible if there is a long autumn, and the plants also produce a few berries sporadically through summer. I grow goji berries in my yard and in my greenhouses and sell the organic plants each spring. I always thought they were non-native, so the first time I found them growing in the wild I thought it was nice that someone had planted them where they could be harvested by the public. Today, I have found them growing wild in dozens of places ranging from high in the mountains to the deep desert and the suburbs. My guess is that birds must have spread the seeds from people who were growing these plants in their yards after the plants became trendy "superberries" for a short time a few years ago. Anyone who has grown goji knows they can be invasive, and they start easily from seed (I grow mine in containers to avoid them becoming a huge hedge). At any rate, however they got spread around the West, I'm always glad to find them and harvest them when hiking or rockhounding.

Lythrum salicaria

(PURPLE LOOSESTRIFE, PURPLE LYTHRUM)

U.S.: Found in all states except Alaska, Arizona, Florida, Georgia, Hawaii, Louisiana, and South Carolina.

CANADA: Found everywhere except Newfoundland and Labrador, Northwest Territories, Nunavut, and Yukon.

EDIBLE PARTS: Leaves, root.

WHEN TO HARVEST: Summer, autumn.

FLOWER COLOR: Purple.

FORM: Multi-stem perennial showy flower typically growing up to three to four feet tall.

HABITAT: Moist soil.

FLAVOR: Mild to slightly bitter.

NOTES: The name is a misnomer because this is not a true loosestrife. This plant is highly invasive. The flowers form a very showy, brightly colored spike. Experts say this plant first arrived in North America by accident in ship ballast, which makes sense because the seeds are primarily dispersed by water. This plant is sometimes called the "purple plague" because it pushes out native species.

Malus domestica

(COMMON APPLE)

U.S.: Found in all states except Alaska, Arizona, Florida, Hawaii, Idaho, Nebraska, North Dakota, Oklahoma, South Dakota, and Texas.

CANADA: Found everywhere except Alberta, Newfoundland and Labrador, Northwest Territories, Nunavut, Saskatchewan, and Yukon.

EDIBLE PARTS: Fruit.

WHEN TO HARVEST: Summer, autumn.

FLOWER COLOR: White.

FORM: Tree.

HABITAT: Streambanks.

FLAVOR: Tart.

NOTES: This is the scientific name of the common grocery store apple, although it is also called other scientific names, including *M. pumila* and *M. sylvestris*. The average American eats an astonishing fifty pounds of apples a year! One apple contains five grams of fiber, making them an excellent source, but most of that fiber is in the peel, so be sure to eat the peel. This is part of the reason why children should be given whole apples to eat instead of applesauce. Wild apples produce smaller fruits than their domesticated siblings. One reason for this is that apples easily produce natural hybrids with other *Malus* species, including crab apples. This is the reason why apple trees are created from cuttings, not seeds (despite what you heard about Johnny Appleseed). Dozens of insect species rely on this species for food and shelter. I've often wondered if the *Malus* name has anything to do with the legend of Snow White and the evil queen's poisoned apple, because it sounds like the word "malice." *Malus* is an unfortunate Latin name for such a beloved fruit.

Malva neglecta

(COMMON MALLOW)

U.S.: Found in all states except Florida, Louisiana, and Mississippi.

CANADA: Found everywhere except Newfoundland and Labrador, Northwest Territories, Nunavut, and Yukon.

EDIBLE PARTS: Leaves, flower, peas.

WHEN TO HARVEST: Spring, summer, autumn.

FLOWER COLOR: Pale lavender, white.

FORM: Spreading, low-growing herbaceous flower.

HABITAT: Disturbed soils, pastures, gardens, roadsides, slopes.

FLAVOR: Mild and slightly sweet.

NOTES: This is one of the most useful plants in the world. The immature seeds form a flat fruit, like a pea, and are delicious raw or parboiled and don't need to be peeled. The whole plant is mucilaginous, meaning it forms a healthy gelatin like substance when crushed, blended, or cooked. The cousin of this plant was used to create the original marshmallow, using the mucilage foam, and that plant is called "marsh mallow." The foam of common mallow is also used to make homemade marshmallows. I use stevia as the sweetener so they are healthy. The leaves are great raw or cooked. The root is a wonderful cheese rennet and is one of the very few plants in the world which produces a rennet that can be used to make hard cheeses instead of just soft cheeses. You can learn to make these simple mallow cheeses in my book *Make Your Own Cheeses.* I grow this plant in my greenhouses in winter because I don't want to be without it, and it is hardy and makes a wonderful winter salad green. The dried roots can also be used to make homemade liquid soap. This is one wild edible I would not be without. Seeds are available at SeedRenaissance.com.

Matricaria discoidea

(PINEAPPLE WEED)

U.S.: Found in all states except Alabama, Florida, Georgia, and Hawaii.

CANADA: Found everywhere except Nunavut.

EDIBLE PARTS: Flowers.

WHEN TO HARVEST: Summer.

FLOWER COLOR: White, yellow.

FORM: Flowering annual herb typically less than twelve inches tall.

HABITAT: Moist disturbed soil, waste places, stream banks.

FLAVOR: Has a sweet pineapple-like fragrance if crushed when young, but the flavor is often slightly bitter, sadly. The Royal Pharmaceutical Society in the United Kingdom says pineapple weed flowers "have an agreeable fruity taste before they are fully ripe, and have been added to salads, as well as being used, either fresh or dried, as an infusion" to drink. They also say this is a rare example of a plant that was native to North America but has now spread invasively in the United Kingdom.

Medicago Species

U.S.: Found in all states.

EDIBLE PARTS: Found everywhere except Newfoundland, Nunavut, Yukon Territory.

EDIBLE PARTS: Leaves, seed.

WHEN TO HARVEST: Summer, autumn.

FLOWER COLOR: Yellow, purple.

FORM: Multi-stemmed flowering herb typically growing up to two feet tall.

HABITAT: Roadsides, lawns, pastures, waste spaces.

FLAVOR: Grass.

NOTES: Black medic is often found in lawns and is more drought-tolerant than regular grass, making it a good no-mow or seldom-mow lawn alternative. It is soft when stepped on and stays green all summer and autumn. Interesti ngly, it also helps make our lawns greener because black medic is symbiotic with Rhizobium bacteria that form nodules on the roots and fix atmospheric nitrogen. Perhaps best of all, every one-half cup (one hundred grams) of black medic leaves contain around twenty-three grams of protein and around twenty-five grams of fiber, which is an astonishing amount of fiber, and everyone needs more fiber. Because I practice herbal medicine, I have searched deeply to find out why this plant is called black medic, but I have never been able to find an answer. The plant is a mild laxative used to ease constipation and tastes best cooked. Alfalfa is called the multivitamin of the herbal world by herbal experts because it is so rich in vitamins, and some people take it every day for this purpose.

EDIBLE SPECIES EXAMPLES:

Medicago lupulina

> **U.S.:** Found in all states.
>
> **CANADA:** Found everywhere except Newfoundland and Labrador, Nunavut, and Yukon.

Medicago polymorpha

> **U.S.:** Found in all states except Colorado, Illinois, Indiana, Iowa, Kansas, Kentucky, Maryland, Minnesota, Nebraska, New Hampshire, North Dakota, South Dakota, West Virginia, and Wisconsin.
>
> **CANADA:** Found in British Columbia, New Brunswick, Ontario, Quebec, and Saskatchewan.

Medicago polymorpha

> **U.S.:** Found in all states.
>
> **CANADA:** Found everywhere except Nunavut.

Medicago lupulina

(BLACK MEDIC)

———

See Medicago Species for details.

Medicago polymorpha

(BURR MEDIC)

See Medicago Species for details.

Medicago sativa

(ALFALFA)

———

See Medicago Species for details.

Melilotus Species

EDIBLE PARTS: *M. albus*, *M. officinalis*: flowers, seedpods, leaves (not dried). *M. indicas:* Leaves (not dried).

WHEN TO HARVEST: Summer.

FLOWER COLOR: Yellow, white.

FORM: Single-stem branching herb with spikes of flowers.

HABITAT: Roadsides, slopes, waste spaces.

FLAVOR: Bitter.

NOTES: It's disappointing that something named sweetclover has such a bitter and drying flavor in the mouth, and I wondered aloud about this one day when hiking. My wife said the old-timers called these plants "sweet clover" because cows who foddered on them gave sweet milk. The things you learn when you are married!

EDIBLE SPECIES EXAMPLES:

Melilotus albus

U.S.: Found in all states.

CANADA: Found everywhere except Nunavut.

NOTES: Some places, including the U.S. Department of Agriculture, have discontinued the use of *Melilotus albus,* preferring instead to classify albus as a subspecies of *Melilotus officinalis*. Not all botanists agree.

Melilotus indicas

U.S.: Found in all states except Alaska, Colorado, Connecticut, Illinois, Indiana, Iowa, Kansas, Maryland, Minnesota, Missouri, Montana, Nebraska, North Dakota, Ohio, South Dakota, Tennessee, and Wyoming.

CANADA: Found in British Columbia, Manitoba, and Nova Scotia.

Melilotus officinalis

U.S.: Found in all states.

CANADA: Found everywhere except Nunavut.

Melilotus albus

(WHITE SWEETCLOVER)

See Melilotus Species for details.

Melilotus indicas

(INDIAN SWEETCLOVER)

See Melilotus Species for details.

Melilotus officinalis

(YELLOW SWEETCLOVER)

See Melilotus Species for details.

Morus alba

(WHITE MULBERRY)

U.S.: Found in all states except Alaska and Nevada.

CANADA: Found in British Columbia, Ontario, and Quebec.

NOTES: There are four *Morus* species found in North America: *M. alba, M. microphylla, M. nigra,* and *M. rubra.* The fruit of all four is edible.

EDIBLE PARTS: Fruit, leaves.

FLOWER COLOR: Green.

FORM: Tree growing fifty feet tall.

HABITAT: Sunny open spaces with regular water.

FLAVOR: Sweet and only slightly tart when fully ripe.

NOTES: These trees were introduced to the West—and indeed the whole country—when settlers attempted to create silkworm industries to manufacture silk. Those efforts survived for a time, and today some of the long-lived trees planted by the pioneers still stand and can often be found in pioneer neighborhoods and early city parks. The berries resemble elongated blackberries. The twigs of *Morus* species, when tender in spring, are somewhat sweet, edible either raw or boiled according to americanforests.org.

Nasturtium officinale

(WATERCRESS)

U.S.: Found in all states except Hawaii and North Dakota.

CANADA: Found everywhere except Newfoundland and Labrador, Northwest Territories, Nunavut, and Yukon.

EDIBLE PARTS: Leaves, seeds.

FLOWER COLOR: White.

FORM: Low-growing perennial flowering herb.

HABITAT: Grows in water or wet soil.

FLAVOR: Hot.

NOTES: When I grew up, the old-timers still ate watercress sandwiches, which is a lost food that should probably make a comeback. The recipe was homemade butter on homemade bread with cress between the slices of bread.

Opuntia Species

U.S.: Found in all states except Alaska, Maine, New Hampshire, and Vermont.

CANADA: Found in Alberta, British Columbia, Manitoba, Ontario, and Saskatchewan.

EDIBLE PARTS: Seeds, fruit, pad (beware thorns).

FLOWER COLOR: Varies.

FORM: Low-growing cactus with pad leaves and thorns.

HABITAT: Desert.

FLAVOR: Fruit is slightly sweet. Pad is mild.

FLOWER COLOR: Varies.

NOTES: There are dozens of species of *Opuntia*, and all are edible. I have many fond memories of *Opuntia*, which I grow in my flower garden, thanks to my oldest grandson, Xander, who digs it out of the river gully and brings it to me because he knows I'm fond of this prickly plant. When I was a youth, my wonderful scoutmaster, Ed Dutson, was intent that we learn Native American and self-reliance skills. He was an expert in both and he had a huge influence on my life. He taught us to harvest *Opuntia* and roast it over the campfire, allowing the spines to be burned off by the fire. We then carefully learned to cut open the roasted pad to avoid the hairlike spines under the skin. The flavor is very mild and actually a lot of fun to eat. Ed Dutson was a giant among men and I am grateful to him for his devotion to scouting, to helping me earn the Eagle Scout rank, and for taking us camping once a month, even in winter. We were a handful and he was patient.

EDIBLE SPECIES EXAMPLES:

Opuntia humifusa

> **U.S.:** Found in all states except Alaska, Arizona, California, Hawaii, Idaho, Nevada, North Dakota, Oregon, Utah, Washington, and Wyoming.
>
> **CANADA:** Found in Ontario.

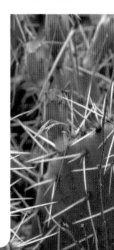

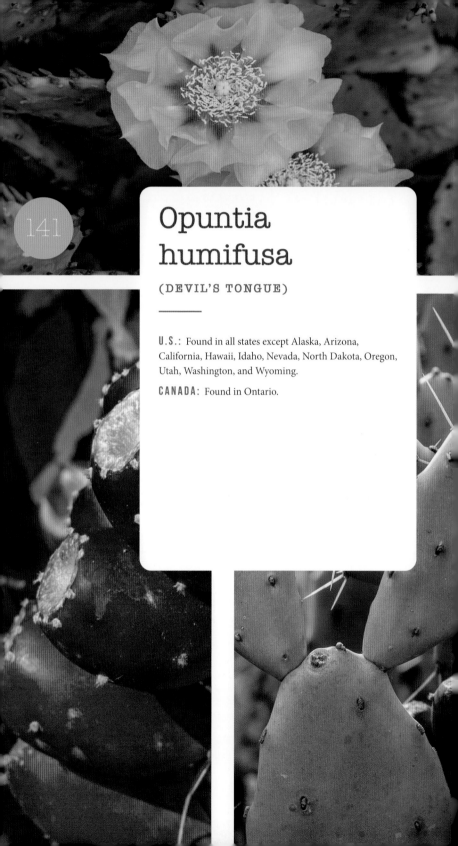

Opuntia humifusa

(DEVIL'S TONGUE)

———

U.S.: Found in all states except Alaska, Arizona, California, Hawaii, Idaho, Nevada, North Dakota, Oregon, Utah, Washington, and Wyoming.

CANADA: Found in Ontario.

Opuntia

(PRICKLY PEAR)

U.S.: Found in all states except Alaska, Maine, New Hampshire, and Vermont.

CANADA: Found in Alberta, British Columbia, Manitoba, Ontario, and Saskatchewan.

NOTES: Several sources, including Mother Earth News, say this species can be divided into the edible beaver-tail type and cholla types, which have round, not flat, pads.

Beware: Do not ingest spines or smaller spines called glochids. As a Scout, we would put these in the campfire to burn off the spines, and then carefully eat the inner flesh. When the Winter Olympics came to Salt Lake City in 2002, I was at a VIP-only dinner for Olympic officials where prickly pear was served along with rattlesnake and other local delicacies.

Oxalis Species

EDIBLE PARTS: Flowers, leaves, roots, seedpods.

WHEN TO HARVEST: Summer, autumn.

FLOWER COLOR: Yellow.

FORM: Low-growing flowering herb.

HABITAT: Shady moist locations.

FLAVOR: Bright lemon.

NOTES: *Oxalis* planted itself in the earthen walls of one of my geothermal greenhouses, and they grow there year-round, so I often get to snack on them. They are a wonderful treat. Woodsorrel is also a possible candidate for no-mow or seldom-mow lawn alternatives. One interesting trait about this plant: it has the unique ability to literally shoot the seeds.

EDIBLE SPECIES EXAMPLES:

Oxalis corniculata

> **U.S.:** Found in all states except Alaska, Colorado, Iowa, Kansas, Minnesota, and Nebraska.

> **CANADA:** Found everywhere except Alberta, New Brunswick, Newfoundland and Labrador, Northwest Territories, Nunavut, and Yukon.

Oxalis stricta

> **U.S.:** Found in all states except Alaska, California, Hawaii, Nevada, Oregon, and Utah.

> **CANADA:** Found everywhere except Alberta, Newfoundland and Labrador, Northwest Territories, Nunavut, and Yukon.

Oxalis corniculata

(CREEPING WOODSORREL)

See Oxalis Species for details.

Oxalis stricta

(YELLOW WOODSORREL)

See Oxalis Species for details.

Panicum Species

EDIBLE PARTS: Seeds.

WHEN TO HARVEST: Late summer, early autumn.

FLOWER COLOR: Green.

FORM: Branching, spreading grass.

HABITAT: Disturbed soils, gardens, fields, roadsides.

FLAVOR: Grain.

NOTES: Witchgrass is a beautiful plant that I find fascinating. I always wait before pulling it out of my garden beds because I love the way it looks, but I don't want to leave it long enough to drop too many seeds, causing me weeding problems the next year in my desert-method hugelkultur gardens. Seeds are ten percent protein but are very small.

EDIBLE SPECIES EXAMPLES:

Panicum capillare

> **U.S.:** Found in all states except Alaska and Hawaii.
>
> **CANADA:** Found everywhere except Newfoundland and Labrador, Northwest Territories, Nunavut, and Yukon.

Panicum dichotomiflorum

> **U.S.:** Found in all states except Alaska, North Dakota, and Wyoming.
>
> **CANADA:** Found in British Columbia, New Brunswick, Nova Scotia, Ontario, and Quebec.

Panicum miliaceum

> **U.S.:** Found in all states except Alaska, Arkansas, Oklahoma, South Carolina, and West Virginia.
>
> **CANADA:** Found everywhere except Newfoundland and Labrador, Northwest Territories, Nunavut, and Yukon.

Panicum capillare

(WITCHGRASS)

See Panicum Species for details.

147

Panicum dichotomiflorum

(FALL PANICUM)

See Panicum Species for details.

Panicum miliaceum

(WILD-PROSO MILLET)

See Panicum Species for details.

Phragmites australis

(COMMON REED)

––––––––

U.S.: Found in all states except Alaska.

CANADA: Found everywhere except Newfoundland and Labrador, Nunavut, and Yukon.

EDIBLE PARTS: Leaves, root, seed, stem.

WHEN TO HARVEST: Spring, summer, autumn.

FLOWER COLOR: Red.

FORM: Spiky grass growing up to thirteen feet high with leaves 2 inches wide and sometimes two feet long.

HABITAT: Grows in water or wet soil.

FLAVOR: Sweet.

NOTES: As with all edible plants harvested from water, harvest only in locations with clean water and rinse thoroughly before eating. Don't harvest from areas where mine tailings poison water with heavy metal deposits, which can be a surprisingly high number of places in the Rocky Mountain West.

Physalis Species

EDIBLE PARTS: Fruit.

WHEN TO HARVEST: Summer.

FLOWER COLOR: White, or yellow and black.

FORM: Flowering perennial typically growing one to two feet tall.

HABITAT: Lawns, gardens, fields, meadows with regular water.

FLAVOR: Mild and bland.

NOTES: These fruits are typically sweetened when eaten or can be added to salsas. Flavor is best when fruits are completely ripe. The berry is covered in a papery shell that dries when the berry is ripe. *P. pruinosa* is a synonym for *P. grisea*. Groundcherries are supposed to be the next big trending superfood—and are also being heavily genetically modified to make them more "fit" for grocery store sales. For seeds of my favorite heirloom pineapple groundcherry, visit SeedRensaissance.com..

EDIBLE SPECIES EXAMPLES:

Physalis heterophylla

> **U.S.:** Found in all states except Alaska, California, Hawaii, and Nevada.
>
> **CANADA:** Found in Nova Scotia, Ontario, and Quebec.

Physalis longifolia

> **U.S.:** Found in all states except Alaska and Hawaii.
>
> **CANADA:** Found in Ontario and Quebec.

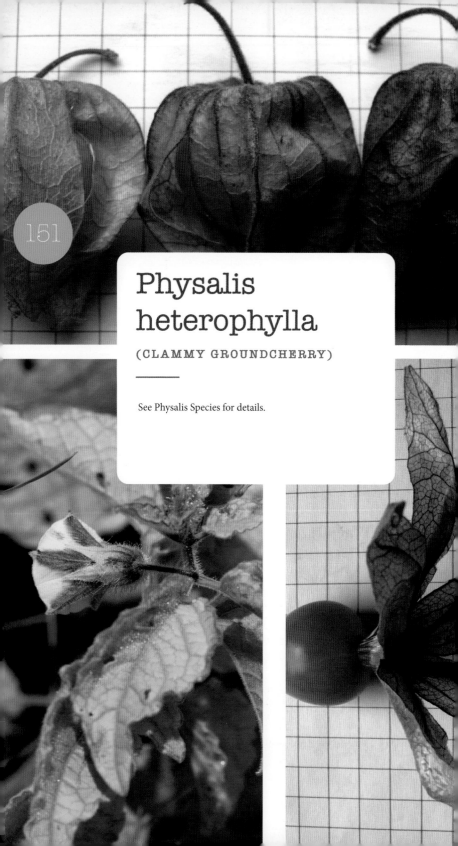

Physalis heterophylla

(CLAMMY GROUNDCHERRY)

See Physalis Species for details.

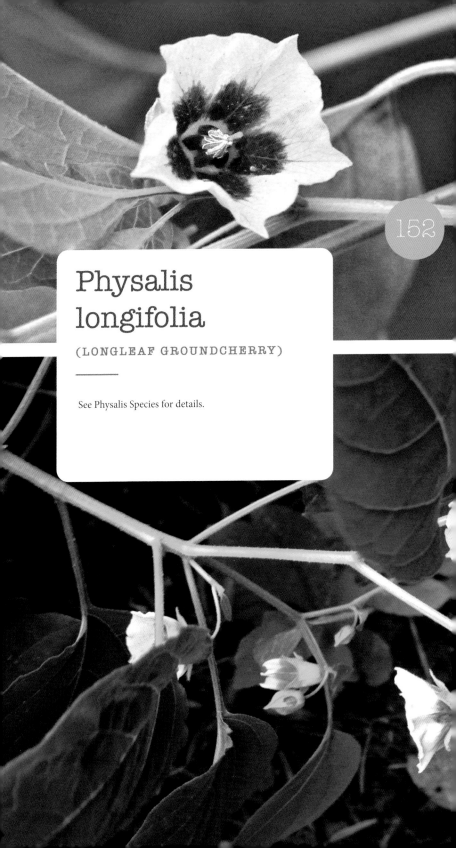

Physalis longifolia

(LONGLEAF GROUNDCHERRY)

See Physalis Species for details.

Plantago Species

EDIBLE PARTS: Leaves, seed.

WHEN TO HARVEST: Spring, summer.

FORM: Low-growing perennial flowering herb.

FLOWER COLOR: *P. major flowers* are green and red. *P. lanceolata* flowers are white

HABITAT: Mountainsides, disturbed soil, gardens, roadsides.

FLAVOR: Mild and grassy.

NOTES: Both plants are also widely used medicinally to treat stings, bites, itching, and other skin irritations. Broadleaf plantain does not tolerate alkaline soil well, and because of this is usually only found at high elevations in the Rocky Mountain West. Narrowleaf plantain tolerates alkaline soil well and is more abundant in the Rocky Mountains for this reason.

EDIBLE SPECIES EXAMPLES:

Plantago lanceolata

    U.S.: Found in all states.

    CANADA: Found everywhere except Newfoundland and Labrador, Northwest Territories, Nunavut, and Yukon.

Plantago major

    U.S.: Found in all states.

    CANADA: Found everywhere except Nunavut.

Plantago lanceolata

(NARROWLEAF PLANTAIN)

See Plantago Species for details.

Plantago major

(BROADLEAF PLANTAIN)

See Plantago Species for details.

Polygonum Species

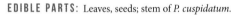

EDIBLE PARTS: Leaves, seeds; stem of *P. cuspidatum*.

WHEN TO HARVEST: Spring, summer, autumn.

FLOWER COLOR: White, purple.

HABITAT: Wet mountainside soils along seeps, streams, and lakes.

FLAVOR: Of all the *Polygonum*, I eat bistort the most. The best part of this plant are the leaves, which are tender and mild. The Native Americans ate the tuberous root of American bistort, which is found about four inches below ground, and when it is washed and peeled it is a beautiful pale pink color and appears to be delicious, until you taste it. The flavor is actually strongly bitter. Cooking and boiling reduces the bitterness a little but not enough to make this root worthwhile.

NOTES: The flower of bistort is striking for its beauty. The first time I ever saw the flower in person was at a campground in the High Uintas and I was enchanted by them. I came home and researched the plants and was pleased to discover it is edible. Today I grow them in my shade garden because I like the flowers so much. They require wet soil and lots of water. For whatever reason I also like the name a lot. *Bistorta bistortoides* is a synonym for *P. bistortoides*. This plant is often found growing among rhizomatous grasses, so tightly inter-growing that you might at first think this is a grassy plant. *P. cuspidatum* plant is highly invasive.

EDIBLE SPECIES EXAMPLES:

Polygonum amphibium

U.S.: Found in all states except Alabama, Florida, Georgia, and Hawaii.

CANADA: Found everywhere except Nunavut.

FORM: Herbaceous perennial water plant.

Polygonum arenastrum

U.S.: Found in all states.

CANADA: Found in all provinces and territories.

FORM: Herbaceous wet-soil annual, sometimes found in dry soils.

Polygonum cuspidatum

U.S.: Found in all states except Alabama, Arizona, Florida, Hawaii, Nevada, New Mexico, North Dakota, Texas, and Wyoming.

CANADA: Found everywhere except Alberta, Newfoundland and Labrador, Northwest Territories, Nunavut, and Yukon.

Polygonum lapathifolium

U.S.: Found in all states except Hawaii.

CANADA: Found everywhere except Nunavut.

FORM: Herbaceous wet soil annual.

Polygonum monspeliensis

U.S.: Found in all states except Illinois, Indiana, Iowa, Kentucky, Missouri, Ohio, Vermont, and West Virginia.

CANADA: Found in Alberta, British Columbia, Manitoba, Ontario, Quebec, Saskatchewan, and Yukon.

Polygonum persicaria

U.S.: Found in all states except Hawaii.

CANADA: Found everywhere except Northwest Territories and Nunavut.

FORM: Herbaceous wet soil annual.

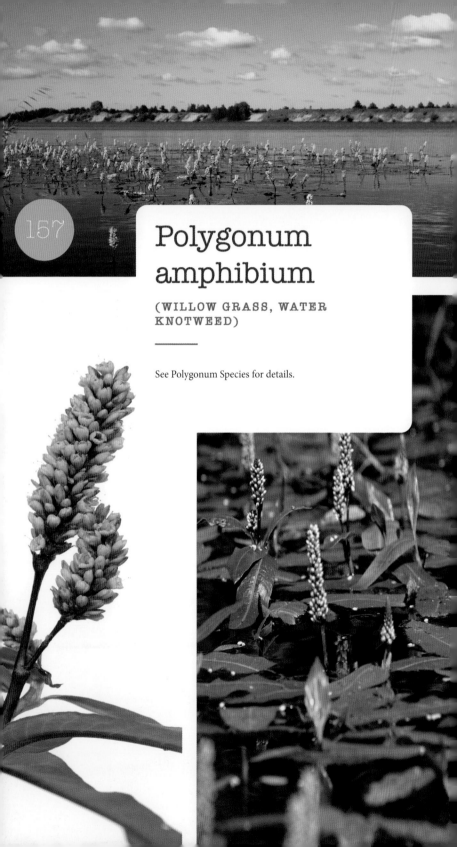

Polygonum amphibium

(WILLOW GRASS, WATER KNOTWEED)

———

See Polygonum Species for details.

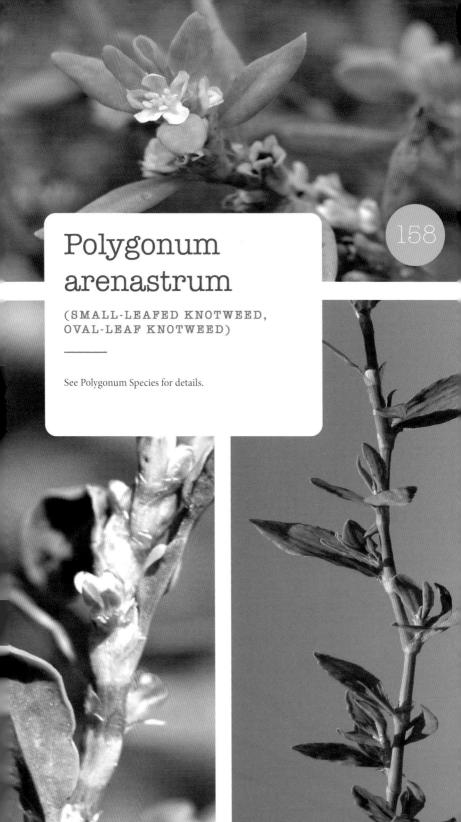

Polygonum arenastrum

(SMALL-LEAFED KNOTWEED, OVAL-LEAF KNOTWEED)

———

See Polygonum Species for details.

Polygonum cuspidatum

(JAPANESE KNOTWEED)

See Polygonum Species for details.

Polygonum lapathifolium

(CURLYTOP KNOTWEED)

———

See Polygonum Species for details.

161

Polypogon monspeliensis

(RABBITFOOT POLYPOGON)

See Polygonum Species for details.

Polygonum persicaria

(SPOTTED LADYSTHUMB)

See Polygonum Species for details.

Portulaca oleracea

(COMMON PURSLANE)

———————

U.S.: Found in all states except Alaska.

CANADA: Found everywhere except Newfoundland and Labrador, Northwest Territories, Nunavut, and Yukon.

EDIBLE PARTS: Leaves, stems, flowers, seed.

WHEN TO HARVEST: Summer, autumn.

FLOWER COLOR: Yellow.

HABITAT: Disturbed soils, roadsides, gardens, fields.

FLAVOR: Lemony, crunchy, and succulent.

NOTES: This is one of the most popular wild edibles wherever it is found growing, and one of my favorites. I like to say it tastes like a crunchy romaine salad with the lemon vinaigrette built right in. The tiny seeds are created in miniature cups on the plant and are highly windborn, so I weed out hundreds of these plants each year, often eating as I go. Sometimes I eat so many of these plants that I can't stand the thought of eating more for a few days!

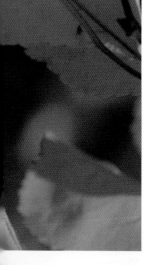

Prunus Species

EDIBLE PARTS: Fruit minus seeds (except *P. dulcis* and *P. fasciculata*)

WHEN TO HARVEST: Summer.

FLOWER COLOR: White, pink.

HABITAT: Stream banks, slopes near water.

FLAVOR: Sweet.

NOTES: For all the species listed here, make sure the fruits are fully ripe for best flavor and sweetness. In his scholarly monograph titled Native American Food Plants, author Daniel E. Moerman says chokecherries had the greatest number of uses by the American Indians of all 1,500 plant species he studied. If *Prunus* fruits are bitter, don't eat them. Nanking cherries and others on this list are now sold commercially. Of all the species listed here, chokecherries are the easiest to find and the most widely used.

EDIBLE SPECIES EXAMPLES:

Prunus americana

> U.S.: Found in all states except Alaska, California, Hawaii, Idaho, Nevada, Oregon, and Texas.
>
> CANADA: Found in Manitoba, Ontario, Quebec, and Saskatchewan.

Prunus pumila

> U.S.: Found in all states except Alabama, Alaska, Arizona, California, Connecticut, Florida, Georgia, Hawaii, Idaho, Louisiana, Mississippi, Missouri, Nevada, New Mexico, North Carolina, Oklahoma, South Carolina, Texas, Virginia, Washington, and West Virginia.
>
> CANADA: Found in Manitoba, New Brunswick, Ontario, Quebec, and Saskatchewan.

Prunus persica

> U.S.: Found in all states except Alaska, Colorado, Hawaii, Minnesota, Montana, Nebraska, Nevada, New Hampshire, North Dakota, South Dakota, Vermont, Washington, and Wyoming.
>
> CANADA: Found in Nova Scotia and Ontario.

Prunus serotina

> U.S.: Found in all states except Alaska, California, Colorado, Hawaii, Idaho, Montana, Nevada, Oregon, South Dakota, Utah, and Wyoming.
>
> CANADA: Found everywhere except Alberta, Manitoba, Newfoundland and Labrador, Northwest Territories, Nunavut, Saskatchewan, and Yukon.

Prunus virginiana

> U.S.: Found in all states except Alabama, Florida, Hawaii, Mississippi, and South Carolina.
>
> CANADA: Found everywhere except Newfoundland and Labrador, Nunavut, and Yukon.
>
> FORM: Herbaceous wet soil annual.

Prunus
americana

(AMERICAN WILD PLUM)

———

See Prunus Species for details.

Prunus pumila

(SANDCHERRY)

See Prunus Species for details.

Prunus persica

(PEACH)

See Prunus Species for details.

Prunus serotina

(BLACK CHERRY)

See Prunus Species for details.

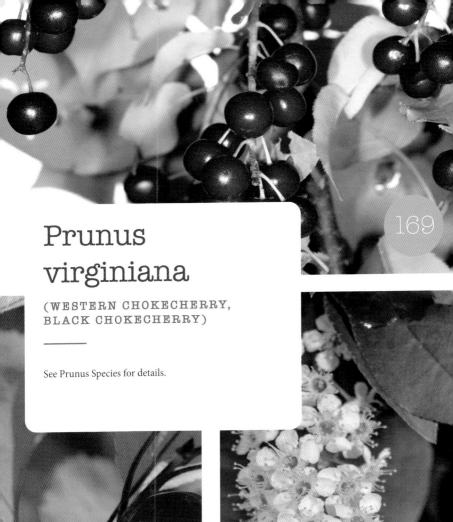

Prunus virginiana

(WESTERN CHOKECHERRY, BLACK CHOKECHERRY)

See Prunus Species for details.

Additional Prunus Species

There are dozens of *Prunus* species all around the country that produce edible wild fruits that can be eaten raw but are most often used to make jams and jellies. The pits of most wild fruits should not be eaten unless you know specifically they are safe, and bitter fruit should always be avoided. Fruit is ripe when it is soft to the touch and has the best flavor in sunny moist locations. Here are some more examples of regional wild edible fruits:

1. *Prunus alabamensis* (Alabama cherry) is found in Alabama, Florida, Georgia, Mississippi, North Carolina, and South Carolina.

2. *Prunus alleghaniensis* (Allegheny plum) is found in the eastern U.S. and the Great Lakes area.

3. *Prunus andersonii* (desert peach) is found in California and Nevada.

4. *Prunus angustifolia* (Chickasaw plum) is found in the entire lower half of the U.S., except desert areas.

5. *Prunus armeniaca* (wild apricot) is found in California, Colorado, Idaho, Illinois, Kansas, Missouri, Montana, Ohio, Oregon, Pennsylvania, and Utah.

6. *Prunus avium* (sweet cherry) is found in western and eastern states of the U.S., as well as British Columbia, Ontario, and areas east of Ontario.

7. *Prunus cerasifera* (cherry plum) is a popular wild fruit found in Ontario, as well as the western and eastern U.S..

8. *Prunus domestica* (European plum) is found in Newfoundland and Labrador, Nova Scotia, Ontario, Quebec, and the western and eastern U.S., as well as Kansas, Louisiana, and Texas.

9. *Prunus gracilis* (Oklahoma plum) is found in its

namesake and all bordering states, as well as Alabama and Louisiana.

10. *Prunus mexicana* (Mexican plum) is found in the central and eastern U.S., but not on the Eastern Seaboard.

11. *Prunus nigra* (Canadian plum) is found in the eastern half of Canada, the Great Lakes region of the U.S. and Canada, and the northern half of the Eastern Seaboard in the U.S.

12. *Prunus susquehanae* (Sesquehanna sandcherry) is found in the same areas as Canadian plums.

13. *Prunus tomentosa* (Nanking cherry) is now widely sold for home landscapes because of its bright red delicious cherries, but is found in the wild in the U.S. in Illinois, Iowa, Maryland, Michigan, Minnesota, Montana, North Carolina, Ohio, Pennsylvania, South Dakota, and Utah, and in Canada in Ontario and Saskatchewan.

14. *Prunus subcordata* (Pacific plum, also called Klamath plum), is found in all west coast states.

Pyrus communis

(COMMON PEAR)

U.S.: Found in all states except Alaska, Arizona, Colorado, Hawaii, Minnesota, Nebraska, Nevada, North Dakota, South Dakota, and Wyoming.

CANADA: Found in British Columbia, Nova Scotia, and Ontario.

EDIBLE PARTS: Fruit.

WHEN TO HARVEST: Summer.

FORM: Tree typically growing up to fifteen feet tall.

FLOWER COLOR: White.

HABITAT: Stream banks, slopes near water.

FLAVOR: Sweet.

NOTES: Wild pear fruits can be quite a bit smaller than commercial varieties. This species is the Latin name of common grocery store pears. Pear trees have been cultivated in Europe for at least a thousand years. One tree can live two hundred and fifty years, so if you think about it, a millennium of cultivation is just four generations of trees. The hardwood of pear trees has also long been used for carving kitchen utensils because it does not take on colors or smells from food.

Raphanus Species

EDIBLE PARTS: Flowers, leaves, seed, seedpod, root.

WHEN TO HARVEST: Summer.

FORM: Single-stem flowering annual or biennial typically growing two feet tall.

FLOWER COLOR: White.

HABITAT: Fields, meadows, roadsides, waste places.

FLAVOR: Radish.

NOTES: These two species often grow together and naturally readily hybridize. Kew Royal Gardens says radishes have been cultivated for so many centuries that no one knows what their natural origin is. Radishes were an important food in Egypt more than three thousand years ago, but did not reach Europe as food until the 1600s.

EDIBLE SPECIES EXAMPLES:

Raphanus raphanistrum

> **U.S.:** Found in all states except Alaska, Arkansas, Nebraska, New Mexico, Oklahoma, South Dakota, Utah, and Wyoming.
>
> **CANADA:** Found everywhere except Northwest Territories, Nunavut, and Yukon.

Raphanus sativus

> **U.S.:** Found in all states.
>
> **CANADA:** Found everywhere except Alberta, Newfoundland and Labrador, Northwest Territories, Nunavut, and Yukon.

Raphanus raphanistrum

(WILD RADISH)

See Raphanus Species for details.

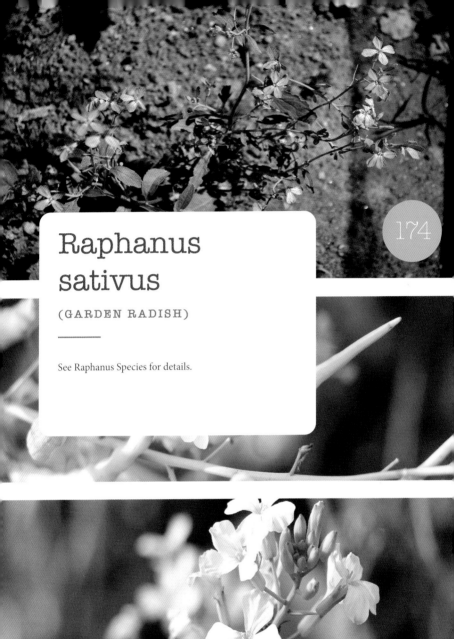

Raphanus sativus

(GARDEN RADISH)

See Raphanus Species for details.

Rhus glabra

(SMOOTH SUMAC)

————

U.S.: Found in all states except Alaska and Hawaii.

CANADA: Found everywhere except New Brunswick, Newfoundland and Labrador, Northwest Territories, Nova Scotia, Nunavut, Prince Edward Island, and Yukon.

EDIBLE PARTS: Fruit.

WHEN TO HARVEST: Autumn.

FORM: Shrubby tree typically growing up to ten feet tall.

FLOWER COLOR: Greenish-red.

HABITAT: Mountainsides.

FLAVOR: Lemony.

NOTES: The velvety fruit is soaked but not boiled to make a lemony drink. Boiling can release toxins, but soaking without boiling is safe. These trees can form an extensive colony from sucker roots. The fruit is rich in vitamin C, which gives it its lemony flavor. The fruits stay on the trees a long time, sometimes through the entire winter.

Ribes Species

U.S.: Found in all states except Hawaii and, Mississippi.

CANADA: Found in all Provinces and Territories.

EDIBLE PARTS: Fruit, flowers, leaves.

WHEN TO HARVEST: Summer.

FORM: Deciduous shrub typically growing two to three feet tall.

FLOWER COLOR: Yellow for R. aureum, white for R. hudsonianum.

HABITAT: Mountainsides.

FLAVOR: Tangy and slightly sweet.

BERRY COLOR: Green, red, black.

NOTES: As a general rule, gooseberries are thorny and currants are not, but there are exceptions. When I go hiking, I use the leaves of *R. cereum* as a kind of lip balm, rubbing the leaves directly on my lips to relieve chapping in the hot summer air. The berries of *R. montigenum* are covered in soft edible hairs. All of these species are naturally high in pectin and can be made into jam or jelly without added pectin (see below for homemade jam recipe).

EDIBLE SPECIES EXAMPLES:

Ribes aureum

> **U.S.:** Found in all states except Alabama, Alaska, Florida, Georgia, Hawaii, Kentucky, Louisiana, Maine, Mississippi, New Hampshire, North Carolina, South Carolina, Virginia, and West Virginia.

> **CANADA:** Found in Alberta, British Columbia, Ontario, Quebec, and Saskatchewan.

Ribes americancum

> **U.S.:** Found in all states except Alabama, Alaska, Arizona, Arkansas, California, Florida, Georgia, Hawaii, Idaho, Kansas, Louisiana, Mississippi, Nevada, North Carolina, Oklahoma, Oregon, South Carolina, Tennessee, Texas, Utah, Virginia, and Washington.

> **CANADA:** Found in Alberta, Manitoba, New Brunswick, Nova Scotia, Ontario, Quebec, and Saskatchewan.

Ribes lacustre

> **U.S.:** Found in all states except Alabama, Arizona, Arkansas, Florida, Georgia, Hawaii, Illinois, Indiana, Iowa, Kansas, Kentucky, Louisiana, Mississippi, Missouri, Nebraska, New Mexico, North Carolina, North Dakota, Ohio, Oklahoma, South Carolina, Tennessee, and Texas.

> **CANADA:** Found everywhere except Nunavut.

Ribes aureum

(GOLDEN CURRANT)

See Ribes Species for details.

Ribes americancum

(AMERICAN BLACK CURRANT)

See Ribes Species for details.

Ribes lacustre

(PRICKLY BLACK CURRANT)

See Ribes Species for details.

Additional Ribes Species

—————

NOTE: There are at least a couple dozen edible currants and gooseberries in North America, but most are specific to regions. Here are some more examples:

1. *Ribes uva-crispa* (European gooseberry) is common in the northeast and the Great Lakes states, even as far west as the Dakotas.

2. *Ribes rubrum* (redcurrant) is generally found in the northern half of the U.S., except Idaho and the Dakotas.

3. Our family makes jam each summer from *Ribes hudsonianum* (western black currant), which is found only in the western U.S., the Great Lakes states, and all of Canada except the Eastern Seaboard.

4. *Ribes inerme* (whitestem gooseberry) is found only in the western United States.

5. *Ribes californicum* (hillside gooseberry) is found only in the Golden State (California).

6. *Ribes niveum* (snow currant) is found in Colorado, Idaho, Nevada, Oregon, and Washington.

7. *Ribes oxyacanthoides* (Canadian gooseberry) is found in the northwest and northern midwest of the U.S., as well as most of Canada.

8. *Ribes nevadense* (Sierra currant) is found in California, Nevada, and Oregon.

9. *Ribes pinetorum* (orange gooseberry) is found in Arizona and New Mexico.

10. *Ribes sanguineum* (redflower currant) is found on the west coast of the U.S. and Canada.

11. *Ribes triste* (red currant) is found in all of Canada and the northern U.S.

12. *Ribes wolfii* (wolf's currant) is found in the Rocky Mountain West and northwest U.S.

13. *Ribes velutinum* (desert gooseberry) is found in the western states of the U.S.

14. *Ribes viburnifolium* (island gooseberry) is found in California.

15. *Ribes quercetorum* (rock gooseberry) is found in Arizona and California.

Dozens of other species are found in only a handful of states each. It is worth finding out which are local to your area.

CURRANT JAM

3 cups rinsed berries with stems removed

Water

3/4 teaspoon powdered stevia extract, 90 percent strength

6 tablespoons birch sugar (xylitol)

Put berries in a saucepan and add enough water to just cover the berries. Add sweeteners. Bring to a boil and simmer on low heat for 40 minutes, stirring often. Turn off heat. Mash remaining berries. Cool until the liquid stops steaming. Taste and add more sweetener if desired. Freeze or refrigerate. Traditional sugar can be used as the sweetener instead of the healthy sweeteners. Start with one cup of traditional sugar and add more to taste. To make a jelly instead of a jam, strain out the berry pulp.

Rosa Species

EDIBLE PARTS: Petals (minus bitter white base), rose hips for tea, seeds (ground up).

WHEN TO HARVEST: Summer, autumn.

FORM: Deciduous shrub typically growing five to eight feet tall.

FLOWER COLOR: Pink, yellow, white, orange.

HABITAT: Mountainsides.

FLAVOR: Slightly sweet.

NOTES: Rosehips are the hard berry-like structures left after the flower has died. The red skin of the berry is high in vitamin C and can be used fresh, dried, or tinctured and is widely sold in health food stores. Ripe rose hips last into winter but should be harvested before they dry and turn brown on the plant. Only the red skin contains the vitamin. The young leaves of *R. rubiginosa* produce an apple-like perfume.

EDIBLE SPECIES EXAMPLES:

Rosa rubiginosa

> **U.S.:** Found in all states except Alaska, Arizona, Florida, Hawaii, Louisiana, Nevada, New Mexico, North Dakota, and South Dakota.

> **CANADA:** Found everywhere except Alberta, Manitoba, Newfoundland and Labrador, Northwest Territories, Nunavut, Saskatchewan, and Yukon.

Rosa woodsii

> **U.S.:** Not found in United States.

> **CANADA:** Found in Alberta, British Columbia, Manitoba, Northwest Territories, Ontario, Quebec, Saskatchewan, and Yukon.

Rosa rubiginosa

(SWEETBRIAR ROSE)

See Rosa Species for details.

Rosa woodsii

(WESTERN WILD ROSE)

See Rosa Species for details.

Rubus Species

U.S.: Found in all states.

CANADA: Found in all Provinces and Territories.

EDIBLE PARTS: Berries, leaves for tea.

WHEN TO HARVEST: Summer.

FORM: Deciduous shrub typically reaching three to four feet tall.

FLOWER COLOR: White, pink, red.

HABITAT: Mountainsides near water.

FLAVOR: Sweet.

BERRY COLOR: Red, black.

NOTES: Most if not all of the *Rubus* fruits mentioned here are wonderful, and the only reason they are not sold in stores is that they are so fragile. Thimbleberry is a prime example of this. The berries are simply delicious, but they tend to fall apart immediately after being picked. Because of this, they can't be commercially handled or shipped, but they are well worth eating in the wild. Some *Rubus* species are hard to tell apart in the wild. *R. procerus* is a synonym for *R. armeniacus*. See below for a homemade jam recipe.

EDIBLE SPECIES EXAMPLES:

Rosa rubiginosa

U.S.: Found in all states except Alaska, Arizona, Florida, Hawaii, Louisiana, Nevada, New Mexico, North Dakota, and South Dakota.

CANADA: Found everywhere except Alberta, Manitoba, Newfoundland and Labrador, Northwest Territories, Nunavut, Saskatchewan, and Yukon.

Rosa woodsii

U.S.: Not found in United States.

CANADA: Found in Alberta, British Columbia, Manitoba, Northwest Territories, Ontario, Quebec, Saskatchewan, and Yukon.

EDIBLE SPECIES EXAMPLES:

Rubus idacus

U.S.: Found in all states except Alabama, Florida, Georgia, Hawaii, Kansas, Kentucky, Louisiana, Mississippi, South Carolina, and Texas.

CANADA: Found in all provinces and territories.

Rubus flagellaris

U.S.: Found in all states except Alaska, Arizona, Colorado, Florida, Hawaii, Idaho, Louisiana, Mississippi, Montana, Nevada, New Mexico, North Dakota, Oregon, South Dakota, Texas, Utah, Washington, and Wyoming.

CANADA: Found in New Brunswick, Nova Scotia, Ontario, and Quebec.

Rubus allegheniensis

U.S.: Found in all states except Alaska, Arizona, California, Colorado, Hawaii, Idaho, Montana, Nevada, New Mexico, North Dakota, Oregon, South Dakota, Utah, Washington, and Wyoming.

CANADA: Found in British Columbia, New Brunswick, Nova Scotia, Ontario, Prince Edward Island, and Quebec.

Rubus armeniacus

U.S.: Found in all states except Alabama, Florida, Georgia, Hawaii, Kansas, Kentucky, Louisiana, Mississippi, South Carolina, and Texas.

CANADA: Found in all provinces and territories.

Rubus occidentails

U.S.: Found in all states except Alaska, Arizona, California, Florida, Hawaii, Idaho, Louisiana, Montana, Nevada, New Mexico, Oregon, Texas, Utah, Washington, and Wyoming.

CANADA: Found in New Brunswick, Ontario, and Quebec.

Rubus flagellaris

(NORTHERN DEWBERRY)

————

See Rubus Species for details.

Rubus allegheniensis

(ALLEGHENY BLACKBERRY)

See Rubus Species for details.

187

Rubus armeniacus

(HIMALAYAN BLACKBERRY)

See Rubus Species for details.

Rubus idacus

(WILD RASPBERRY)

———

See Rubus Species for details.

Rubus occidentalis

(BLACK RASPBERRY)

———

See Rubus Species for details.

Additional Rubus Species

NOTES: The fruits of all *Rubus* species are edible according to Eattheweeds.com. Many grocery store favorites are in this genus, including raspberries, blackberries, boysenberry, loganberries, dewberries, and more. Many people don't know that wild raspberries, for example, come in several colors in nature, including white, gold, black, and purple in addition to the common red. Our family grows several colors and varieties. Most, however, are found only in small regions and sometimes only one state. Here are some more examples:

1. *Rubus argutus* (sawtooth blackberry) is found in the East and South of the U.S.

2. *Rubus arcticus* (Arctic raspberry) is found in all parts of Canada and a handful of northern U.S. states.

3. *Rubus canadensis* (smooth blackberry) is found in the eastern U.S. and Canada.

4. *Rubus parviflorus* (thimbleberry), one of my favorites, is found in the western U.S. and Canada, as well as the Great Lakes area of the U.S. and Canada.

5. *Rubus cuneifolius* (sand blackberry) is found in eastern and southern U.S. states.

6. *Rubus aboriginum* (garden dewberry) is found in California and the southeast quadrant of the U.S., except Florida.

7. *Rubus alaskensis* (Alaska blackberry) is found only in, you guessed it, it's namesake state.

8. One of the most beautifully named edibles on the planet, cloudberries (*Rubus chamaemorus*) are found in all parts of Canada and in Maine, Minnesota, New Hampshire, and New York.

9. *Rubus audax* (Tampa blackberry) is found only in

Florida, Georgia, North Carolina, and South Carolina.

10. The temptingly monikered "delicious raspberry" (*Rubus deliciosus*) is found only in Colorado, New Mexico, Oklahoma, and Wyoming.

11. *Rubus felix* (woodland dewberry) is found in Kentucky, Massachusetts, New York, Virginia, and West Virginia.

12. *Rubus glaucifolius* (San Diego raspberry) is only found in California and Oregon.

13. *Rubus persistens* (persistent blackberry) is found in the Southern United States.

14. *Rubus mirus* (marvel dewberry) is found only in Florida and Mississippi.

15. *Rubus ulmifolius* (elmleaf dewberry) is found only in California, Nevada, and Oregon .

16. *Rubus setosus* (setose blackberry) is found in the Great Lakes and East Coast areas of the U.S. and Canada.

WILD BERRY JAM

3 cups rinsed berries with stems removed

Water

1/2 teaspoon powdered stevia extract, 90 percent strength

4 tablespoons birch sugar (xylitol)

Put berries in a saucepan and add enough water to just cover the berries. Add sweeteners. Bring to a boil and simmer on low heat for 25–30 minutes, stirring often. Turn off heat. Mash berries. Cool until the liquid stops steaming. Taste and add more sweetener if desired. Freeze or refrigerate. Traditional sugar can be used as the sweetener instead of the healthy sweeteners. Start with one cup of traditional sugar and add more to taste. To make a jelly instead of a jam, strain out the berry pulp.

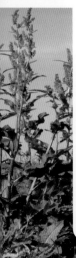

Rumex Species

EDIBLE PARTS: Leaves, root, seed, stem

WHEN TO HARVEST: Spring, summer

FORM: Multi-stem herb typically growing up to 3 feet tall

FLOWER COLOR: Green

HABITAT: Roadsides, wastelands, disturbed soils, fields, pastures

FLAVOR: Lemony

NOTES: Young leaves have the best flavor. Most people know dock from the spikes of red seeds that appear in summer. Curly dock is widely eaten as a wild forage food and is valued for adding to green smoothies for its lemony flavor. You probably know it because of the showy spikes of rust-red seeds that form a tall display beginning in late summer. Dock leaves are particularly attacked by grasshoppers, which eat big holes in the leaves, but they continue to put out smaller leaves all summer, which are great for eating fresh. *Rumex* are wind pollinated and thus don't draw many insect visitors beyond grasshoppers.

EDIBLE SPECIES EXAMPLES:

Rumex acetosella

U.S.: Found in all states.

CANADA: Found everywhere except Northwest Territories and Nunavut.

Rumex crispus

U.S.: Found in all states.

CANADA: Found everywhere except Nunavut.

Rumex obtusifolius

U.S.: Found in all states except Nevada, North Dakota, and Wyoming.

CANADA: Found in British Columbia, Newfoundland and Labrador, New Brunswick, Nova Scotia, Ontario, Prince Edward Island, and Quebec.

Rumex
acetosella

(SHEEP SORREL)

See Rumex Species for details.

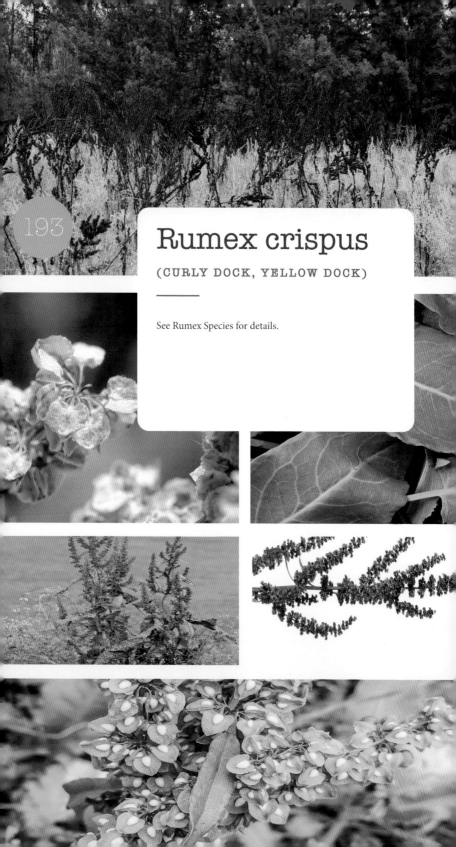

193

Rumex crispus

(CURLY DOCK, YELLOW DOCK)

See Rumex Species for details.

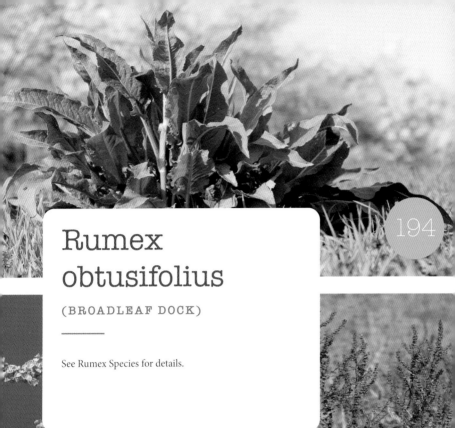

Rumex
obtusifolius

(BROADLEAF DOCK)

————

See Rumex Species for details.

194

Sagittaria cuneata

(WAPATO, ARUMLEAR ARROWHEAD)

U.S.: Found in all states except Alabama, Arkansas, Florida, Georgia, Hawaii, Kentucky, Louisiana, Maryland, Mississippi, Missouri, North Carolina, South Carolina, Tennessee, Virginia, and West Virginia.

CANADA: Found everywhere except Newfoundland and Labrador and Nunavut.

EDIBLE PARTS: Tuber.

WHEN TO HARVEST: Spring, summer, autumn.

FORM: Aquatic herb that typically grows two feet tall.

FLOWER COLOR: White.

HABITAT: Grows in water or wet soil.

FLAVOR: Starchy and slightly nutty.

NOTES: Harvest only from clean and unpolluted water; rinse thoroughly before eating. The flowers are stunning in their beauty. After reaching the Pacific Ocean, the Lewis and Clark expedition spent the bitter winter of 1805–06 at Fort Clatsop, near Astoria, Oregon. Among the foods they ate through the winter "was the starch-rich tuber of the Indian potato or Wapato (*Sagittaria cuneata*)," says the U.S. Forest Service. "The tubers have a potato-like texture but more of the flavor of water chestnuts when boiled or roasted to remove their slightly bitter taste when raw. Arrowhead tubers grow in muddy soil underwater and were harvested by Indians using sticks or with their bare feet (once freed, the tubers float to the surface to be gathered)." The plant is also called "arrowhead" because of the shape of its leaves.

Salsola tragus

(RUSSIAN THISTLE)

U.S.: Found in all states except Alaska and Florida.

CANADA: Found everywhere except Northwest Territories, Nunavut, and Yukon.

EDIBLE PARTS: Young leaves, young shoots, young stems, seeds.

WHEN TO HARVEST: Spring.

FORM: Annual tumbleweed typically growing two to three feet tall and two to three feet wide.

FLOWER COLOR: White, pink.

HABITAT: Desert.

FLAVOR: Mild and slightly salty. *Salsola* means salty.

NOTES: Because thistles are so invasive, especially in disturbed soils, we might as well seek them out in spring to eat them as our revenge for being such a pest plant. They are very spiny, so avoid this plant except in its young stages. Be aware this plant is highly variable in its appearance in nature and identification can be hampered depending on soil, water, and other conditions.

Sambucus Species

EDIBLE PARTS: Ripe berries.

WHEN TO HARVEST: Autumn.

FORM: Blue elderberry is a deciduous shrubby tree growing up to twenty feet tall. Red and black elderberries are typically much smaller, growing up to 3 feet tall. Some sources still argue that red elderberries are poisonous. I'm not sure where this rumor comes from; they have been widely eaten for centuries!

FLOWER COLOR: White.

HABITAT: Mountainsides.

FLAVOR: Slightly sweet.

NOTES: Elderberry plants have toothed, pinnate, and lanceolate leaves. Branches are dotted with raised lenticels. Red elderberry is generally a much shorter plant than the blue or black species. Elderberries are easily found in the mountains and are widely used medicinally. See the end of this section for a homemade elderberry syrup recipe.

EDIBLE SPECIES EXAMPLES:

Rumex acetosella

> **U.S.:** Found in all states except Alaska.
>
> **CANADA:** Found everywhere except Alberta, Newfoundland and Labrador, Northwest Territories, Nunavut, Saskatchewan, and Yukon.

Rumex crispus

> **U.S.:** Found in all states except Alabama, Arkansas, Florida, Hawaii, Kansas, Louisiana, Mississippi, Nebraska, Oklahoma, South Carolina, and Texas.
>
> **CANADA:** Found everywhere except Newfoundland and Labrador, Northwest Territories, and Nunavut.

Sambucus nigra

(BLUE ELDERBERRY)

————

See Sambucus Species for details.

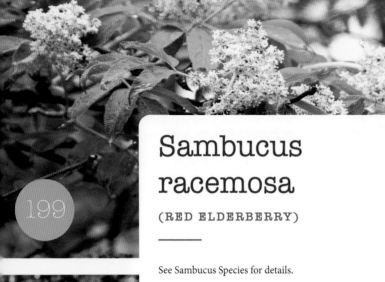

Sambucus racemosa

(RED ELDERBERRY)

———

See Sambucus Species for details.

ELDERBERRY SYRUP

———————————————————————————

3 cups fresh blue elderberries, rinsed and stems removed

Water

3/4 teaspoon stevia powder extract, 90 percent strength

1/2 cup birch sugar (xylitol)

Remove the largest stems. Tiny stems do not need to be removed, because stems and pulp will be removed later. Put berries in a saucepan and add enough water to just cover the berries. Bring to a boil and then simmer on low until water is reduced by half, approximately 30–40 minutes, stirring frequently. The berries will turn colors as they heat up, changing from blue to black to red and finally to purple. Turn off heat and strain or sieve berries from liquid. Discard pulp. Cool the liquid until it stops steaming and then refrigerate. Syrup will slowly thicken in the fridge, becoming syrup after about 24 hours. Use on pancakes or vanilla ice cream, or add 1 teaspoon to a cup of water for a delicious drink. You can substitute the stevia and birch sugar in this recipe for 1 cup of regular white refined sugar if desired. Add a little more or less sweetener as desired.

Secale cereale

(CEREAL RYE)

———————

U.S.: Found in all states except Hawaii, Oklahoma, and West Virginia.

CANADA: Found everywhere except Newfoundland and Labrador and Nunavut.

EDIBLE PARTS: Grain.

WHEN TO HARVEST: Summer.

FORM: Single-stemmed grass typically growing up to 4 feet tall.

FLOWER COLOR: Green.

HABITAT: Roadsides, fields, dry wastelands.

FLAVOR: Grain.

NOTES: This is perhaps the single most important wild edible in North America. The settlers are believed to have brought it here from Europe because it so easily self-seeds, and it has been very happy in its new home. Today, cereal rye grows rampantly across hundreds of thousands of acres, providing an important food supply for birds and critters, but there is also plenty for humans who want to harvest it. Rye can be used on its own for bread, or mixed with wheat or other grains. There is enough wild rye growing in the West to provide critical winter food stores for probably the entire population—if it were harvested. Like all grains, rye must be harvested in July or it begins to disappear, knocked to the ground by winds and taken by birds. The grain plants itself in early spring, pressed to the ground and covered in its own cozy blanket of straw laid flat by the winter snows. At our house, we harvest this grain from the wild every year by hand. Keep in mind that cereal rye, like all wild edibles, must be legally harvested, with permission if on lands you don't own. This important foodstuff helped sustain the pioneers and has since sustained itself, a sort of latent food security surrounding us on a massive scale. Everyone has seen it, but few recognize its value or history.

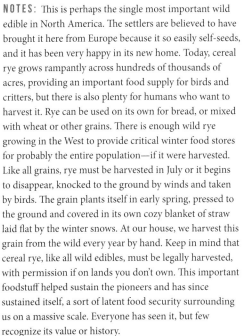

Setaria pumila

(YELLOW FOXTAIL)

U.S.: Found in all states except Alaska.

CANADA: Found everywhere except Newfoundland and Labrador, Northwest Territories, Nunavut, and Yukon.

EDIBLE PARTS: Seed.

WHEN TO HARVEST: Summer.

FORM: Annual bunch grass growing up to three feet tall.

FLOWER COLOR: Green.

HABITAT: Roadsides, fields, dry wastelands.

FLAVOR: Grain.

NOTES: The grain is an important source of food for certain squirrels and many songbirds. There are many *Setaria* species and it is likely that some of them may also be used for edible seeds and grains, though edibility is unknown. One of the great things about this plant is its wide availability.

Sonchus Species

EDIBLE PARTS: Young leaves, root, stem.

WHEN TO HARVEST: Summer.

FORM: *S. arvensis* is perennial, while *S. asper* and *S. oleraceus* are annual. All grow two to four feet tall.

FLOWER COLOR: Yellow.

HABITAT: Disturbed soils, roadsides, wastelands.

FLAVOR: Mild. If the flavor of the greens is bitter, you have waited until they are too old to pick them. If you raise rabbits, they are also fond of eating these plants. S. arvensis first arrived in the U.S. in Pennsylvania in 1814, likely as contamination from Europe. Today it is listed as an invasive noxious weed in more than a dozen states. The horizontal roots of one plant can stretch out as much as six feet! When eating this plant, the key is to get it early in the season while it is tender. This plant provides forage for sheep, cattle, and pronghorn and is an important food source for rabbits in the wild.

EDIBLE SPECIES EXAMPLES:

Sonchus arvensis

U.S.: Found in all states except Alabama, Arizona, Arkansas, Florida, Georgia, Hawaii, Oklahoma, and South Carolina.

CANADA: Found everywhere except Newfoundland and Labrador and Nunavut.

Sonchus asper

U.S.: Found in all states.

CANADA: Found everywhere except Northwest Territories and Nunavut.

Sonchus oleraceus

U.S.: Found in all states.

CANADA: Found everywhere except Newfoundland and Labrador, Nunavut, and Yukon.

Sonchus arvensis

(SOWTHISTLE)

See Sonchus Species for details.

Sonchus asper

(SPINY SOWTHISTLE)

204

See Sonchus Species for details.

Sonchus oleraceus

(COMMON SOWTHISTLE)

———

See Sonchus Species for details.

Sorbus scopulina

(EUROPEAN MOUNTAIN ASH)

U.S.: Found everywhere except Alabama, Arizona, Arkansas, Florida, Georgia, Kansas, Kentucky, Louisiana, Mississippi, Missouri, Nebraska, Nevada, New Mexico, North Carolina, Oklahoma, South Dakota, Tennessee, Texas, and Virginia.

CANADA: Found everywhere except Manitoba, Northwest Territories, Nunavut, and Yukon.

EDIBLE PARTS: Berries.

WHEN TO HARVEST: August, September.

FORM: Tree up to fifty feet tall.

FLOWER COLOR: White.

HABITAT: Tolerates a wide variety of soils and conditions.

FLAVOR: Acidic.

NOTES: The fruits can be made into jam. As with all wild fruits, don't overeat or you may get a sour stomach. The tree produces large amounts of fruit, which hang together in bunches, making it easier to harvest enough for jam. The tree was brought to North America from the U.K. and Europe. According to the U.K.'s Woodland Trust, this tree was once widely planted by houses as a protection against witches. The color red was considered to be the best color for fighting evil, and so this tree—also called rowan, with its bright red berries—"has long been associated with magic and witches. Its old Celtic name is 'fid na ndruad,' which means wizards' tree. In Ireland, it was planted near houses to protect them against spirits, and in Wales rowan trees were planted in churchyards. Cutting down a rowan was considered taboo in Scotland. The wood was used for stirring milk, to prevent it curdling, and as a pocket charm against rheumatism. It was also used to make divining rods." So, if you plant this tree, you might not get any trick-or-treaters, I guess.

Sorghum Species

EDIBLE PARTS: Seeds can be used cooked or ground for flour.

WHEN TO HARVEST: Late summer.

FORM: Perennial grass typically growing about three feet tall.

FLOWER COLOR: Green.

HABITAT: Disturbed soils, roadsides, fields.

FLAVOR: Grain.

NOTES: This plant spreads by rhizome and also by seeds, which spread easily. In many parts of the world, farmers consider this plant to be invasive and aggressive. Johnsongrass was historically a folk remedy for blood and urinary disorders, according to Purdue University.

EDIBLE SPECIES EXAMPLES:

Sorghum bicolor

    U.S.: Found in all states except Alaska and West Virginia.

    CANADA: Found in Ontario and Quebec.

Sorghum halpense

    U.S.: Found in all states except Alaska, Maine, and Minnesota.

    CANADA: Found in Ontario.

Sorghum bicolor

(WILD GRAIN SORGHUM)

See Sorghum Species for details.

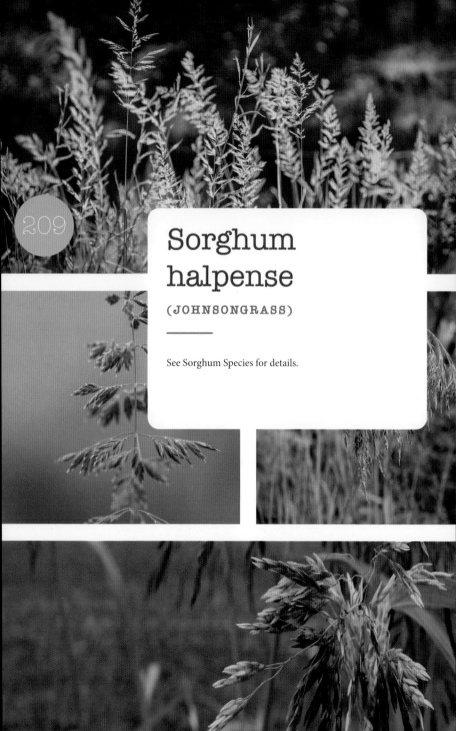

Sorghum halpense

(JOHNSONGRASS)

See Sorghum Species for details.

Stellaria media

(CHICKWEED)

U.S.: Found in all states.

CANADA: Found everywhere except Nunavut.

EDIBLE PARTS: Leaves and seeds, raw or cooked. The seeds are eighteen percent protein and six percent fat.

WHEN TO HARVEST: Summer.

FORM: Low-growing flowering herb.

FLOWER COLOR: White.

HABITAT: Moist shady mountainside locations.

FLAVOR: Mild.

NOTES: This plant can be invasive, but I have allowed it to naturalize in one of my greenhouses so I can eat it during winter and early spring, because where I live in the desert, this plant grows wild only in the high mountains. I have even been criticized for selling the seeds for these plants on my website, SeedRenaissance.com, because they are so invasive in some places in the world. But if I didn't plant them from seed, I wouldn't have them to eat since they are not common in my area. They have a great lemony flavor.

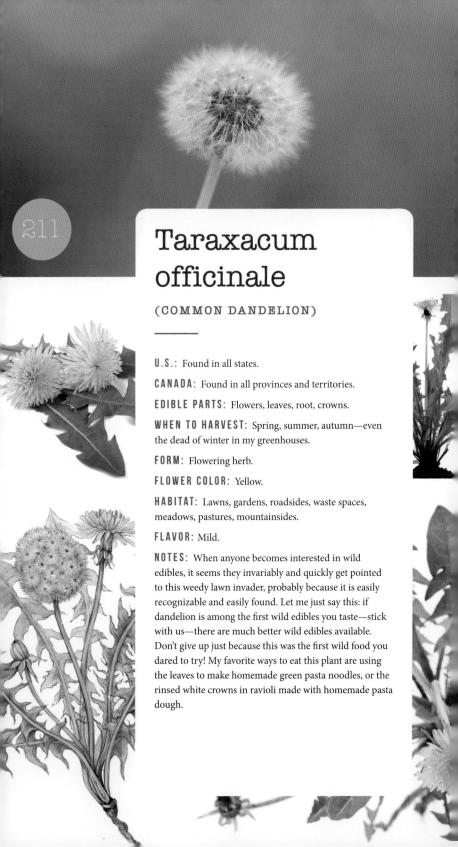

Taraxacum officinale

(COMMON DANDELION)

—

U.S.: Found in all states.

CANADA: Found in all provinces and territories.

EDIBLE PARTS: Flowers, leaves, root, crowns.

WHEN TO HARVEST: Spring, summer, autumn—even the dead of winter in my greenhouses.

FORM: Flowering herb.

FLOWER COLOR: Yellow.

HABITAT: Lawns, gardens, roadsides, waste spaces, meadows, pastures, mountainsides.

FLAVOR: Mild.

NOTES: When anyone becomes interested in wild edibles, it seems they invariably and quickly get pointed to this weedy lawn invader, probably because it is easily recognizable and easily found. Let me just say this: if dandelion is among the first wild edibles you taste—stick with us—there are much better wild edibles available. Don't give up just because this was the first wild food you dared to try! My favorite ways to eat this plant are using the leaves to make homemade green pasta noodles, or the rinsed white crowns in ravioli made with homemade pasta dough.

Thlaspi arvense

(FIELD PENNYCRESS)

———

U.S.: Found in all states except Alabama and Hawaii.

CANADA: Found everywhere except Nunavut.

EDIBLE PARTS: Young leaves, seed.

WHEN TO HARVEST: Spring.

FORM: Annual branching flowering herb typically growing two feet tall.

FLOWER COLOR: White.

HABITAT: Lawns, gardens, roadsides, waste spaces, meadows, pastures, mountainsides.

FLAVOR: Bitter when raw, but cooking makes the leaves more mild. Known for its coin-like seeds, which give this plant its name. The leaves can be mistaken for chicory, especially in the early season. The leaves have some garlic flavor.

Tragopogon Species

EDIBLE PARTS: Root, leaves, flower buds.

FORM: Biennial single-stemmed flowering herb.

FLOWER COLOR: Yellow.

HABITAT: Fields, disturbed soils, pastures, gardens.

FLAVOR: Mild. The flower buds are slightly sweet with a sticky resin that I love. The roots are somewhat like skinny parsnips.

NOTES: I grow these in my greenhouse because the plants are so useful and tasty and I can get larger roots for harvesting in the spring when I grow them indoors. The wild roots sometimes have stunted roots because of heavy clay soil, but not always. Root flavor can also be affected by how much water the wild plants get. I love these plants and eat them often. The early flower buds, while they are small, have a sweet resin on them and eating them is a treat, but they are fibrous as they get closer to opening the flower petals.

EDIBLE SPECIES EXAMPLES:

Tragopogon dubius

    U.S.: Found in all states except Alabama, Florida, Hawaii, Mississippi, and South Carolina.

    CANADA: Found everywhere except Newfoundland and Labrador and Nunavut.

Tragopogon pratensis

    U.S.: Found in all states except Alabama, Alaska, Arkansas, Florida, Hawaii, Louisiana, Mississippi, North Carolina, North Dakota, South Carolina, and South Dakota.

    CANADA: Found everywhere except Newfoundland and Labrador, Northwest Territories, Nunavut, and Yukon.

Tragopogon porrifolius

    U.S.: Found in all states except Alabama, Alaska, Louisiana, Minnesota, Mississippi, North Dakota, and South Carolina.

    CANADA: Found everywhere except Newfoundland and Labrador, Northwest Territories, Nunavut, Saskatchewan, and Yukon.

Tragopogon dubius

(YELLOW SALSIFY)

————

See Tragopogon dubius for details.

Tragopogon pratensis

(GOAT'S BEARD, MEADOW SALSIFY)

———

See Tragopogon dubius for details.

Tragopogon porrifolius

(SALSIFY)

See Tragopogon dubius for details.

Trifolium Species

EDIBLE PARTS: Flowers, leaves, roots.

FORM: Spring, summer, autumn.

FLOWER COLOR: White, red.

HABITAT: Lawns, roadsides, waste spaces, pastures.

FLAVOR: Mild.

EDIBLE SPECIES EXAMPLES:

Trifolium hybridum

> **U.S.:** Found in all states except Texas.
>
> **CANADA:** Found everywhere except Nunavut.

Trifolium incarnatum

> **U.S.:** Found in all states except Alaska, Arizona, Colorado, Indiana, Nevada, Utah, and Wyoming.
>
> **CANADA:** Found in British Columbia, Manitoba, and Ontario.
>
> **NOTES:** The seeds of this species are edible and are often eaten sprouted. The flowers are edible according to ediblewildfood.com, but others disagree. The dried flowers can be used for tea but not eaten, according to practicalplants.org.

Trifolium repens

> **U.S.:** Found in all states.
>
> **CANADA:** Found everywhere except Nunavut.

Trifolium pratense

> **U.S.:** Found in all states.
>
> **CANADA:** Found everywhere except Nunavut.

Trifolium hybridum

(ALSIKE CLOVER)

See Trifolium Species for details.

218

Trifolium incarnatum

(CRIMSON CLOVER)

See Trifolium Species for details.

Trifolium repens

(WHITE CLOVER, DUTCH CLOVER)

See Trifolium Species for details.

Trifolium pratense

(RED CLOVER)

See Trifolium Species for details.

Additional Trifolium Species

1. *Trifolium fucatum* (bull clover) is found on the West Coast and in Michigan. Leaves and seeds are edible.

2. *Trifolium obtusiflorum* (clammy clover) seeds are edible; found in California and Oregon.

3. *Trifolium lupinaster* (lupine clover) is found only in Alaska. The leaves are edible.

4. *Trifolium subterraneum* (subterranean clover) leaves are edible. Found on the West Coast of the U.S. and in British Columbia, as well as around the Gulf Coast and in Massachusetts and New Jersey.

5. *Trifolium macrocephalum* (largehead clover) is found on the West Coast of the U.S. and in Idaho. The leaves are edible.

Typha Species

EDIBLE PARTS: Flowers, leaves, pollen, root, seed, stem.

WHEN TO HARVEST: Spring, summer, autumn.

FORM: Tall single-time grass typically growing six to ten feet tall.

FLOWER COLOR: Brown/green.

HABITAT: Grows in water or wet soil.

FLAVOR: Where to begin? The inner stems of cattails should be sold in grocery stores because they are unbelievably delicious—crunchy, fresh, mildly sweet. They are one of my all-time favorite wild foods. But be sure to get them in spring, because by the heat of summer they have become fibrous. The only caution is that you want to make sure you get them clean, because they are often growing in standing water. Make sure the water is clean, and be sure to rinse them carefully.

NOTES: Both the settlers and the Native Americans ground the dried pollen and seeds as flour and mixed them with wheat flour to make any number of baked goods, especially in times when wheat flour was scarce or expensive. The roots were also used fresh and dried, and when dried, were often ground for flour. I'll be honest—I never get much past the stems because I find the inner stems to be addictively wonderful to eat. And one stem provides a huge amount to eat.

EDIBLE SPECIES EXAMPLES:

Typha angustifolia

> **U.S.:** Found in all states except Alabama, Alaska, Arizona, Florida, Georgia, Hawaii, Texas, and Utah.
>
> **CANADA:** Found everywhere except Alberta, Newfoundland and Labrador, Northwest Territories, Nunavut, and Yukon.

Typha glauca

> **U.S.:** Found in all states except Alaska, Arizona, Hawaii, Idaho, Kansas, Louisiana, Nebraska, Nevada, New Mexico, North Dakota, Oklahoma, Tennessee, and Texas.
>
> **CANADA:** Found in Manitoba, New Brunswick, Ontario, Quebec, and Saskatchewan.

Typha latifolia

> **U.S.:** Found in all states.
>
> **CANADA:** Found everywhere except Newfoundland and Labrador and Nunavut.

Typha angustifolia

(NARROWLEAF CATTAIL)

See Typha Species for details.

Typha glauca

(HYBRID CATTAIL)

See Typha Species for details.

Typha latifolia

(BROADLEAF CATTAIL)

See Typha Species for details.

Urtica dioica

(STINGING NETTLE)

U.S.: Found in all states except Arkansas and Hawaii.

CANADA: Found everywhere except Nunavut.

EDIBLE PARTS: Leaves.

WHEN TO HARVEST: Spring, summer, autumn.

FORM: Tall single-stem branching flower.

FLOWER COLOR: Green/tan.

HABITAT: Shady moist soils on mountainsides and slopes.

FLAVOR: Mild.

NOTES: Yes, I know, you have questions. Eat stinging nettle? Yes. This plant has changed my life! It is a strong natural antihistamine that controls my allergies and asthma far better than anything from the pharmacy. I doubt anyone in the world has eaten more stinging nettle leaves than I have. I grow stinging nettle in my gardens because I need it as medicine, and I eat it on almost every hike I go on, even in Europe. Let me begin by saying that the needles of the plant are located on the main stem and the leaf stems. To harvest a leaf, I pinch off the leaf just above the leaf stem, without touching the stem. Some large leaves also have a few needles on the main leaf vein, so I fold these leaves before eating. I have been stung so many times by nettle that I no longer have a reaction to it at all. The cure for nettle is nettle. If you get stung, *don't* itch or scratch. Once you irritate the skin, the swelling and itching are much more difficult to get rid of. But if you don't touch your skin, you can eat one or two leaves and all sting, swelling, and scratching will be gone in three to four minutes. Stinging nettle is also a widely sold and widely used medicinal, so you can still use it to control

your allergies even if you don't want to harvest it wild—but it is so widely available you might as well harvest it. Or grow your own. I sell the seeds at SeedRenaissance.com. Everyone in our family uses this. The little kids (our grandkids) even call me from school when they have itchy eyes to request that I bring leaves to them from the garden. Me bringing a bag of fresh nettle leaves to the school for a fifth grader raised some eyebrows! All the little kids pick them and eat them on our hikes too. I tell you all this to give you courage. Both the settlers and the American Indians ate nettle as a common vegetable, and I'm sure they also used it medicinally. Let me end by saying that I was not exaggerating a bit when I said this plant has changed my life! My allergies have landed me in the emergency room on many occasions (because I would stop breathing) before herbal medicine gave me control of my health. If I had to pick only one wild plant to harvest the rest of my life, stinging nettle would be my choice, without question or hesitation!

Vaccinium Species

EDIBLE PARTS: Berries.

WHEN TO HARVEST: Summer, autumn.

FORM: Perennial shrub.

FLOWER COLOR: Varies.

HABITAT: Shady understory plant usually found in forests where it is moist and temperatures are cooler.

FLAVOR: Sweet when fully ripe, some have tartness.

NOTES: Summer drought and late spring frosts can dramatically reduce the number of berries that appear, but they are never prolific. Because of this, they are like saskatoons—they are generally eaten on the spot instead of gathered for home use.

Addtional Vaccinium Species

Blueberries, cranberries, huckleberries, lingonberries, and bilberries are all *Vaccinium* species. All *Vaccinium* in North America have edible berries and most are delicious. They are found in all parts of Canada and every state except North Dakota and Nebraska.

1. *Vaccinium alaskaense* (Alaska blueberry) is found in its namesake state, Oregon, and Washington.

2. *Vaccinium angustifolium* (lowbush blueberry) is found in all eastern U.S. states above the Gulf Coast, as well as all of eastern Canada.

3. *Vaccinium arboreum* (farkleberry) is found in the lower right quadrant of the U.S.

4. *Vaccinium boreale* (northern blueberry) is found in all land east of and including New York and Quebec.

5. *Vaccinium caesariense* (New Jersey blueberry) is found along the Eastern Seaboard from Florida to Maine.

6. Hawaii boasts three species found only on the islands: *Vaccinium reticulatum, Vaccinium calycinum, Vaccinium dentatum* (all called ohelo blueberries).

7. *Vaccinium cespitosum* (dwarf bilberry) is found in all of Canada except Nunavut, the western U.S., and the north-most U.S. states.

8. *Vaccinium corymbosum* (highbush blueberry) is found in the eastern U.S. and Canada, the Gulf Coast states, British Columbia, and Oregon.

9. *Vaccinium crassifolium* (creeping blueberry) is found from Georgia to Virginia.

10. *Vaccinium darrowii* (Darrow's blueberry) is found in Alabama, Georgia, Florida, Mississippi, and Louisiana.

11. *Vaccinium deliciosum* (cascade bilberry) is found on the West Coast and in Idaho and British Columbia.

12. *Vaccinium elliottii* (Elliott's blueberry) is found from Texas to Virginia.

13. *Vaccinium erythrocarpum* (southern mountain cranberry) is found in the southern states above Florida.

14. *Vaccinium formosum* (southern blueberry) is found from Alabama and Florida through New Jersey.

15. *Vaccinium fuscatum* (black highbush blueberry) is found in the eastern half of the U.S. and lower Midwest states.

16. *Vaccinium hirsutum* (hairy blueberry) is found in Georgia, North Carolina, and Tennessee.

17. *Vaccinium macrocarpon* (cranberry) is found on the West Coast and in British Columbia, Northwest Territories, and the eastern half of the U.S. above the Gulf Coast.

18. *Vaccinium membranaceum* (thinleaf huckleberry) is found in all of the western U.S. states and Canada.

19. *Vaccinium myrsinites* (shiny blueberry) is found in most Gulf Coast states.

20. *Vaccinium myrtilloides* (velvetleaf huckleberry) is found in most of Canada and the upper right quadrant of the United States.

21. *Vaccinium myrtillus* (whortleberry) is found in the western parts of Canada and the U.S.

22. *Vaccinium ovalifolium* (oval-leaf blueberry) is found in the western and eastern portions of Canada, as well as the north-most U.S. states.

23. *Vaccinium ovatum* (California huckleberry) is found on the West Coast and in British Columbia.

24. *Vaccinium oxycoccos* (small cranberry) is found in all of Canada and the eastern U.S., as well as Idaho, Oregon,

and Washington.

25. *Vaccinium pallidum* (Blue Ridge blueberry) is found in the eastern U.S. and Ontario.

26. *Vaccinium parvifolium* (red huckleberry) is found on the West Coast and in Alaska and British Columbia.

27. *Vaccinium scoparium* (grouse whortleberry) is found in the western U.S., as well as Alberta and British Columbia.

28. *Vaccinium simulatum* (upland highbush blueberry) is found from Florida to the Great Lakes states.

29. *Vaccinium stamineum* (deerberry) is found in Ontario, the lower right quadrant of the U.S., and U.S. states east of the Great Lakes.

30. *Vaccinium tenellum* (small black blueberry) is found in the Gulf Coast states.

31. *Vaccinium uliginosum* (bog blueberry) is found in all of Canada, the western U.S., and most northern U.S. states touching the Canadian border.

32. *Vaccinium virgatum* (smallflower blueberry) is found from Texas to the Carolinas.

33. *Vaccinium vitis-idaea* (lingonberry) is found in all of Canada, as well as the Great Lakes states and all states east of New York.

Viola canadensis

(CANADIAN WHITE VIOLET)

U.S.: Found in all states except California, Florida, Hawaii, Kansas, Louisiana, Mississippi, Missouri, Nevada, Oklahoma, and Texas.

CANADA: Found everywhere except Newfoundland and Labrador and Nunavut.

EDIBLE PARTS: Young leaves, flower buds, flower.

WHEN TO HARVEST: Spring.

FORM: Low-growing showy flower.

FLOWER COLOR: Purple/blue.

HABITAT: Garden, mountainsides, meadows.

FLAVOR: Mild. Flowers are slightly sweet.

NOTES: Flowers have a nice fragrance. In the Eastern U.S., this plant is sometimes considered a weed because it invades lawns. People in the West only wish flowers other than dandelions would invade their lawns. According to Lake Forest College research, a poultice of the leaves was used to treat headaches by Native Americans. It's worth a try.

Vitis Species

U.S.: Found in all states except Alaska and Hawaii.

CANADA: Found in Manitoba, Ontario, Quebec, New Brunswick, and Nova Scotia.

EDIBLE PARTS: Berries, leaves.

WHEN TO HARVEST: Summer.

FORM: Perennial vine.

FLOWER COLOR: Green/white.

HABITAT: Mountain canyons near water.

FLAVOR: Grape. Just like backyard grapes (of which these are a cousin), the berries are best when eaten fully ripe on the vine. Wild grape plants can be difficult to find.

EDIBLE SPECIES EXAMPLES:

Vitis Aestivalis

> **U.S.:** Found in all states except Alaska, Arizona, Colorado, Hawaii, Idaho, Montana, New Mexico, North Dakota, Oregon, South Dakota, Utah, Washington, and Wyoming.
>
> **CANADA:** Found in Ontario.

Vitis riparia

> **U.S.:** Found in all states except Alabama, Alaska, Arizona, California, Florida, Georgia, Hawaii, Idaho, Mississippi, Nevada, New Mexico, South Carolina, and Utah.
>
> **CANADA:** Found in Manitoba, Ontario, Quebec, New Brunswick, and Nova Scotia.

Vitis Aestivalis

(SUMMER GRAPE)

See Vitis Species for details.

Vitis riparia

(RIVERBANK GRAPE)

————

See Vitis Species for details.

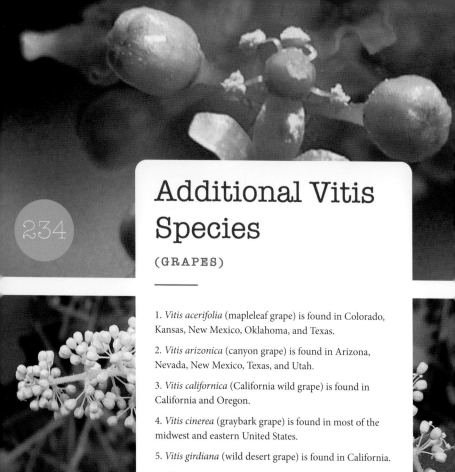

Additional Vitis Species

(GRAPES)

1. *Vitis acerifolia* (mapleleaf grape) is found in Colorado, Kansas, New Mexico, Oklahoma, and Texas.

2. *Vitis arizonica* (canyon grape) is found in Arizona, Nevada, New Mexico, Texas, and Utah.

3. *Vitis californica* (California wild grape) is found in California and Oregon.

4. *Vitis cinerea* (graybark grape) is found in most of the midwest and eastern United States.

5. *Vitis girdiana* (wild desert grape) is found in California.

6. *Vitis labrusca* (fox grape) is found in Utah and also from the Great Lakes down to Louisiana and east, except Florida.

7. *Vitis monticola* (sweet mountain grape) is found in New Mexico and Texas.

8. *Vitis mustangensis* (mustang grape) is found in Alabama, Arkansas, Louisiana, Oklahoma, and Texas.

9. *Vitis palmata* (catbird grape) is found from the Great Lakes down to Texas and over to Florida.

10. *Vitis rotundifolia* (muscadine grape) is found in the lower right quadrant of the United States.

11. *Vitis rupestris* (sand grape) is found in California and most states in the lower right quadrant of the United States.

12. *Vitis vinifera* (wine grape) is found on the West Coast and in Alabama, Florida, Idaho, Texas, Utah, and most of the north half of the eastern seaboard.

13. *Vitis vulpina* (frost grape) is found in Ontario and most of the Midwest and eastern U.S. states.

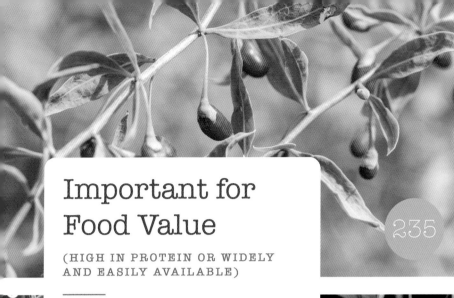

Important for Food Value

(HIGH IN PROTEIN OR WIDELY AND EASILY AVAILABLE)

Amaranthus retroflexus (Redroot Pigweed, Redroot Amaranth)

Arctium minus (Lesser Burdock)

Asclepias syriaca (Common Milkweed)

Avena fatua (Wild oat)

Avena sativa (Common oat)

Barbarea vulgaris (Garden Yellowrocket)

Brassica juncea (Brown mustard)

Brassica napus (Rape mustard)

Brassica nigra (Black mustard)

Brassica rapa (Field mustard)

Capsella bursa-pastoris (Shepherd's Purse)

Cardaria draba (Whitetop, Hoary Cress)

Celtis occidentalis (Common Hackberry)

Chamerion angustifolium (Fireweed)

Chenopodium album (Lamb's-quarters, Wild Spinach)

Chorispora tenella (Blue mustard)

Cichorium intybus (Chicory)

Cyperus erythrorhizos (Redroot flatsedge)

Cyperus esculentus (Yellow Nutsedge)

Cyperus odoratus (Fragrant flatsedge)

Cyperus schweinitzii (Schweinitz's flatsedge)

Cyperus squarrosus (Bearded flatsedge)

Daucus carota (Wild carrot)

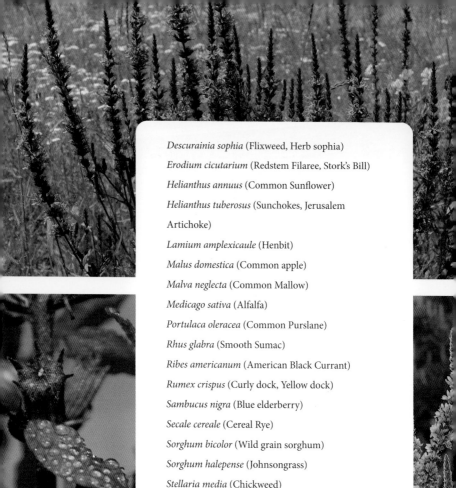

Descurainia sophia (Flixweed, Herb sophia)

Erodium cicutarium (Redstem Filaree, Stork's Bill)

Helianthus annuus (Common Sunflower)

Helianthus tuberosus (Sunchokes, Jerusalem Artichoke)

Lamium amplexicaule (Henbit)

Malus domestica (Common apple)

Malva neglecta (Common Mallow)

Medicago sativa (Alfalfa)

Portulaca oleracea (Common Purslane)

Rhus glabra (Smooth Sumac)

Ribes americanum (American Black Currant)

Rumex crispus (Curly dock, Yellow dock)

Sambucus nigra (Blue elderberry)

Secale cereale (Cereal Rye)

Sorghum bicolor (Wild grain sorghum)

Sorghum halepense (Johnsongrass)

Stellaria media (Chickweed)

Taraxacum officinale (Common Dandelion)

Tragopogon dubius (Yellow Salsify)

Tragopogon pratensis (Goat's Beard, Meadow Salsify)

Trifolium pratense (Red clover)

Urtica dioica (Stinging Nettle)

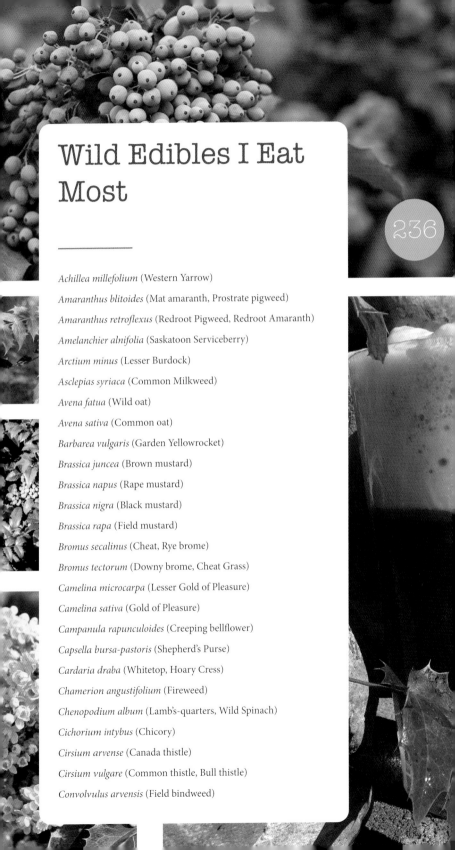

Wild Edibles I Eat Most

236

Achillea millefolium (Western Yarrow)

Amaranthus blitoides (Mat amaranth, Prostrate pigweed)

Amaranthus retroflexus (Redroot Pigweed, Redroot Amaranth)

Amelanchier alnifolia (Saskatoon Serviceberry)

Arctium minus (Lesser Burdock)

Asclepias syriaca (Common Milkweed)

Avena fatua (Wild oat)

Avena sativa (Common oat)

Barbarea vulgaris (Garden Yellowrocket)

Brassica juncea (Brown mustard)

Brassica napus (Rape mustard)

Brassica nigra (Black mustard)

Brassica rapa (Field mustard)

Bromus secalinus (Cheat, Rye brome)

Bromus tectorum (Downy brome, Cheat Grass)

Camelina microcarpa (Lesser Gold of Pleasure)

Camelina sativa (Gold of Pleasure)

Campanula rapunculoides (Creeping bellflower)

Capsella bursa-pastoris (Shepherd's Purse)

Cardaria draba (Whitetop, Hoary Cress)

Chamerion angustifolium (Fireweed)

Chenopodium album (Lamb's-quarters, Wild Spinach)

Cichorium intybus (Chicory)

Cirsium arvense (Canada thistle)

Cirsium vulgare (Common thistle, Bull thistle)

Convolvulus arvensis (Field bindweed)

Crepis capillaris (Smooth Hawksbeard)

Daucus carota (Wild carrot)

Descurainia sophia (Flixweed, Herb sophia)

Equisetum arvense (Horsetail grass)

Fragaria vesca (Woodland, Alpine, or Wild Strawberry)

Fragaria virginiana (Virginia strawberry)

Galium aparine (Cleavers, Goosegrass)

Geranium bicknellii (Bicknell's cranesbill)

Helianthus annuus (Common Sunflower)

Helianthus tuberosus (Sunchokes, Jerusalem Artichoke)

Hibiscus trionum (Venice Mallow)

Hordeum jubatum (Foxtail Barley, Squirrel-tail Grass)

Kochia scoparia (Kochia)

Lamium amplexicaule (Henbit)

Lepidium perfoliatum (Clasping Pepperweed)

Lycium barbarum (Gojiberry, Wolfberry)

Malus domestica (Common apple)

Malva neglecta (Common Mallow)

Medicago sativa (Alfalfa)

Melilotus officinalis (Yellow sweetclover)

Panicum capillare (Witchgrass)

Plantago lanceolata (Narrowleaf plantain)

Portulaca oleracea (Common Purslane)

Prunus virginiana (Western Chokecherry, Black chokecherry)

Rhus glabra (Smooth Sumac)

Ribes lacustre (Prickly Black Currant)

Ribes uva-crispa European gooseberries

Ribes rubrum

Ribes hudsonianum (Western Black Currants)

Ribes triste (Red currants)

Rosa woodsii (Western Wild Rose)

Rubus idaeus (Wild raspberries)

Rubus parviflorus (Thimbleberries)

Rumex crispus (Curly dock, Yellow dock)

Sambucus nigra (Blue elderberry)

Sambucus racemosa (Red Elderberry)

Secale cereale (Cereal Rye)

Stellaria media (Chickweed)

Taraxacum officinale (Common Dandelion)

Tragopogon dubius (Yellow Salsify)

Tragopogon pratensis (Goat's Beard, Meadow Salsify)

Tragopogon porrifolius (Salsify)

Typha angustifolia (Narrowleaf cattail)

Typha glauca (Hybrid cattail)

Typha latifolia (Broadleaf cattail)

Urtica dioica (Stinging Nettle)

Vaccinium vitis-idaea (Lingonberry)

Fruits & Berries

———

Amelanchier alnifolia (Saskatoon Serviceberry)

Celtis occidentalis (Common Hackberry)

Cornus canadensis (Creeping dogwood)

Cornus sericea (Western dogwood)

Crataegus chrysocarpa (Red haw tree)

Crataegus succulenta (Fleshy hawthorn)

Elaeagnus angustifolia (Russian Olive)

Elaeagnus commutata (Silverberry)

Fragaria vesca (Woodland, Alpine, or Wild Strawberry)

Fragaria virginiana (Virginia strawberry)

Gaultheria hispidula (Creeping Snowberry)

Lycium barbarum (Gojiberry, Wolfberry)

Malus domestica (Common apple)

Morus alba (White mulberry)

Physalis heterophylla (Clammy groundcherry)

Physalis longifolia (Longleaf groundcherry)

Prunus americana (American Wild Plum)

Prunus pumila (Sandcherry)

Prunus persica (Peach)

Prunus serotina (Black Cherry)

Prunus virginiana (Western Chokecherry, Black chokecherry)

Prunus alabamensis (Alabama cherry)

Prunus alleghaniensis (Allegheny plum)

Prunus andersonii (Desert peach)

Prunus angustifolia (Chickasaw plum)

Prunus armeniaca (Wild apricots)

Prunus avium (Sweet cherries)

Prunus cerasifera (Prunus avium)

Prunus domestica (European plums)

Prunus gracilis (Oklahoma plum)

Prunus mexicana (Mexican plums)

Prunus nigra (Canadian plums)

Prunus susquehanae (Sesquehana sandcherry)

Prunus tomentosa (Nanking cherry)

Pyrus communis (Common pear)

Rhus glabra (Smooth Sumac)

Ribes aureum (Golden Currant)

Ribes americanum (American Black Currant)

Ribes lacustre (Prickly Black Currant)

Ribes uva-crispa European gooseberries

Ribes rubrum

Ribes hudsonianum (Western Black Currants)

Ribes inerme (Whitestem gooseberries)

Ribes californicum (Hillside gooseberry)

Ribes niveum (Snow currant)

Ribes oxyacanthoides (Canadian gooseberry)

Ribes nevadense (Sierra currants)

Ribes pinetorum (Orange gooseberries)

Ribes sanguineum (Redflower currants)

Ribes triste (Red currants)

Ribes wolfii (Wolf's currant)

Ribes velutinum (Desert gooseberry)

Ribes viburnifolium (Island gooseberry)

Ribes quercetorum (Rock gooseberry)

Rubus idaeus (Wild raspberries)

Rubus flagellaris (Northern dewberry)

Rubus allegheniensis (Allegheny blackberry)

Rubus armeniacus (Himalayan blackberry)

Rubus occidentalis (Black raspberries)

Rubus argutus (Sawtooth blackberry)

Rubus arcticus (Arctic raspberry)

Rubus canadensis (Smooth blackberry)

Rubus parviflorus (Thimbleberries)

Rubus cuneifolius (Sand blackberry)

Rubus aboriginum (Garden dewberry)

Rubus alaskensis (Alaska blackberry)

Rubus chamaemorus (Cloudberries)

Rubus audax (Tampa blackberry)

Rubus deliciosus (Delicious Raspberry)

Rubus felix (Woodland dewberries)

Rubus glaucifolius (San Diego raspberry)

Rubus persistens (Persistent blackberries)

Rubus mirus (Marvel dewberries)

Rubus ulmifolius (Elmleaf dewberries)

Rubus setosus (Setose blackberry)

Sambucus racemosa (Red Elderberry)

Vaccinium alaskaense (Alaska blueberry)

Vaccinium angustifolium (Lowbush blueberry)

Vaccinium arboreum (Farkleberry)

Vaccinium boreale (Northern blueberry)

Vaccinium caesariense (New Jersey blueberry)

Vaccinium reticulatum (Ohelo blueberries)

Vaccinium calycinum (Ohelo blueberries) (again)

Vand accinium dentatum (all called Ohelo blueberries)

Vaccinium cespitosum (Dwarf bilberry)

Vaccinium corymbosum (Highbush blueberry)

Vaccinium crassifolium (Creeping blueberry)

Vaccinium darrowii (Darrow's blueberry)

Vaccinium deliciosum (Cascade bilberry)

Vaccinium elliottii (Elliott's blueberry)

Vaccinium erythrocarpum (Southern mountain cranberry)

Vaccinium formosum (Southern blueberry)

Vaccinium fuscatum (black highbush blueberry)

Vaccinium hirsutum (Hairy blueberry)

Vaccinium macrocarpon (Cranberry)

Vaccinium membranaceum (Thinleaf huckleberry)

Vaccinium myrsinites (Shiny blueberry)

Vaccinium myrtilloides (Velvetleaf huckleberry)

Vaccinium myrtillus (Whortleberry)

Vaccinium ovalifolium (Oval-leaf blueberry)

Vaccinium ovatum (California huckleberry)

Vaccinium oxycoccos (Small cranberry)

Vaccinium pallidum (Blue Ridge blueberry)

Vaccinium parvifolium (Red huckleberry)

Vaccinium scoparium (Grouse whortleberry)

Vaccinium simulatum (Upland highbush blueberry)

Vaccinium stamineum (Deerberry)

Vaccinium tenellum (Small black blueberry)

Vaccinium uliginosum (Bog blueberry)

Vaccinium virgatum (Smallflower blueberry)

Vaccinium vitis-idaea (Lingonberry)

Vitis aestivalis (Summer Grape)

Vitis riparia (Riverbank grape)

Vitis acerifolia (Mapleleaf grape)

Vitis arizonica (Canyon grape)

Vitis californica (California wild grape)

Vitis cinerea (Graybark grape)

Vitis girdiana (Wild desert grape)

Vitis labrusca (Fox grape)

Vitis monticola (Sweet mountain grape)

Vitis mustangensis (Mustang grape)

Vitis palmata (Catbird grape)

Vitis rotundifolia (Muscadine grape)

Vitis rupestris (Sand grape)

Vitis vinifera (Wine grape)

Vitis vulpina (Frost grape)

Significant Grains & Seeds

Aegilops cylindrica (Jointed goatgrass)

Amaranthus albus (Tumble pigweed)

Amaranthus blitoides (Mat amaranth, Prostrate pigweed)

Amaranthus hybridus (Slim Amaranth)

Amaranthus powellii (Powell's amaranth)

Amaranthus retroflexus (Redroot Pigweed, Redroot Amaranth)

Amaranthus tuberculatus (Roughfruit Amaranth)

Avena fatua (Wild oat)

Avena sativa (Common oat)

Barbarea vulgaris (Garden Yellowrocket)

Brassica juncea (Brown mustard)

Brassica napus (Rape mustard)

Brassica nigra (Black mustard)

Brassica rapa (Field mustard)

Bromus japonicus (Japanese brome, Field brome)

Bromus secalinus (Cheat, Rye brome)

Bromus tectorum (Downy brome, Cheat Grass)

Camelina microcarpa (Lesser Gold of Pleasure)

Camelina sativa (Gold of Pleasure)

Capsella bursa-pastoris (Shepherd's Purse)

Cenchrus longispinus (Longspine sandbur)

Descurainia pinnata (Western Tansy Mustard)

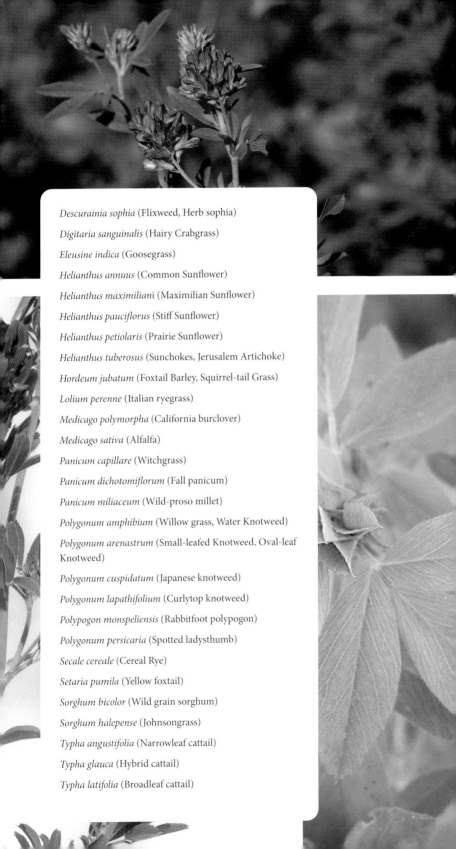

Descurainia sophia (Flixweed, Herb sophia)

Digitaria sanguinalis (Hairy Crabgrass)

Eleusine indica (Goosegrass)

Helianthus annuus (Common Sunflower)

Helianthus maximiliani (Maximilian Sunflower)

Helianthus pauciflorus (Stiff Sunflower)

Helianthus petiolaris (Prairie Sunflower)

Helianthus tuberosus (Sunchokes, Jerusalem Artichoke)

Hordeum jubatum (Foxtail Barley, Squirrel-tail Grass)

Lolium perenne (Italian ryegrass)

Medicago polymorpha (California burclover)

Medicago sativa (Alfalfa)

Panicum capillare (Witchgrass)

Panicum dichotomiflorum (Fall panicum)

Panicum miliaceum (Wild-proso millet)

Polygonum amphibium (Willow grass, Water Knotweed)

Polygonum arenastrum (Small-leafed Knotweed, Oval-leaf Knotweed)

Polygonum cuspidatum (Japanese knotweed)

Polygonum lapathifolium (Curlytop knotweed)

Polypogon monspeliensis (Rabbitfoot polypogon)

Polygonum persicaria (Spotted ladysthumb)

Secale cereale (Cereal Rye)

Setaria pumila (Yellow foxtail)

Sorghum bicolor (Wild grain sorghum)

Sorghum halepense (Johnsongrass)

Typha angustifolia (Narrowleaf cattail)

Typha glauca (Hybrid cattail)

Typha latifolia (Broadleaf cattail)

Nuts

Corylus cornuta (Beaked hazelnut)

Juglans nigra (Black walnut)

Significant Roots & Tubers

Arctium minus (Lesser Burdock)

Calypso bulbosa (Fairy Slipper)

Cichorium intybus (Chicory)

Cyperus erythrorhizos (Redroot flatsedge)

Cyperus esculentus (Yellow Nutsedge)

Cyperus odoratus (Fragrant flatsedge)

Cyperus schweinitzii (Schweinitz's flatsedge)

Cyperus squarrosus (Bearded flatsedge)

Daucus carota (Wild carrot)

Malva neglecta (Common Mallow)

Raphanus raphanistrum (Wild radish)

Raphanus sativus (Garden Radish)

Rumex acetosella (Sheep Sorrel)

Rumex crispus (Curly dock, Yellow dock)

Rumex obtusifolius (Broadleaf dock)

Sagittaria cuneata (Wapato, Arumleaf Arrowhead)

Taraxacum officinale (Common Dandelion)

Tragopogon dubius (Yellow Salsify)

Tragopogon pratensis (Goat's Beard, Meadow Salsify)

Tragopogon porrifolius (Salsify)

Typha angustifolia (Narrowleaf cattail)

Typha glauca (Hybrid cattail)

Typha latifolia (Broadleaf cattail)

Trees/Shrubs/ Bushes

Acer negundo (Box Elder Maple)

Amelanchier alnifolia (Saskatoon Serviceberry)

Artemisia frigida (Fringed Sagebrush)

Celtis occidentalis (Common Hackberry)

Cornus canadensis (Creeping dogwood)

Cornus sericea (Western dogwood)

Corylus cornuta (Beaked hazelnut)

Crataegus chrysocarpa (Red haw tree)

Crataegus succulenta (Fleshy hawthorn)

Elaeagnus angustifolia (Russian Olive)

Elaeagnus commutata (Silverberry)

Juglans nigra (Black walnut)

Lycium barbarum (Gojiberry, Wolfberry)

Malus domestica (Common apple)

Morus alba (White mulberry)

Prunus americana (American Wild Plum)

Prunus pumila (Sandcherry)

Prunus persica (Peach)

Prunus serotina (Black Cherry)

Prunus virginiana (Western Chokecherry, Black chokecherry)

Prunus alabamensis (Alabama cherry)

Prunus alleghaniensis (Allegheny plum)

Prunus andersonii (Desert peach)

Prunus angustifolia (Chickasaw plum)

Prunus armeniaca (Wild apricots)

Prunus avium (Sweet cherries)

Prunus cerasifera (Prunus avium)

Prunus domestica (European plums)

Prunus gracilis (Oklahoma plum)

Prunus mexicana (Mexican plums)

Prunus nigra (Canadian plums)

Prunus susquehanae (Sesquehana sandcherry)

Prunus tomentosa (Nanking cherry)

Pyrus communis (Common pear)

Rhus glabra (Smooth Sumac)

Ribes aureum (Golden Currant)

Ribes americanum (American Black Currant)

Ribes lacustre (Prickly Black Currant)

Ribes uva-crispa European gooseberries

Ribes rubrum

Ribes hudsonianum (Western Black Currants)

Ribes inerme (Whitestem gooseberries)

Ribes californicum (Hillside gooseberry)

Ribes niveum (Snow currant)

Ribes oxyacanthoides (Canadian gooseberry)

Ribes nevadense (Sierra currants)

Ribes pinetorum (Orange gooseberries)

Ribes sanguineum (Redflower currants)

Ribes triste (Red currants)

Ribes wolfii (Wolf's currant)

Ribes velutinum (Desert gooseberry)

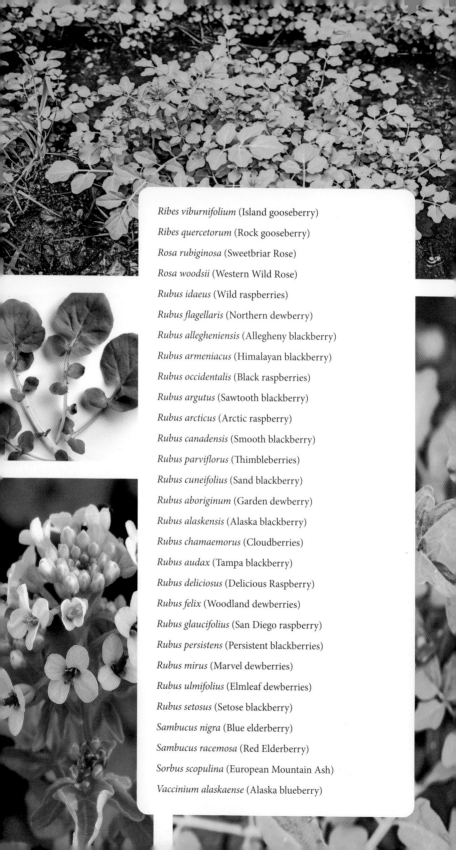

Ribes viburnifolium (Island gooseberry)

Ribes quercetorum (Rock gooseberry)

Rosa rubiginosa (Sweetbriar Rose)

Rosa woodsii (Western Wild Rose)

Rubus idaeus (Wild raspberries)

Rubus flagellaris (Northern dewberry)

Rubus allegheniensis (Allegheny blackberry)

Rubus armeniacus (Himalayan blackberry)

Rubus occidentalis (Black raspberries)

Rubus argutus (Sawtooth blackberry)

Rubus arcticus (Arctic raspberry)

Rubus canadensis (Smooth blackberry)

Rubus parviflorus (Thimbleberries)

Rubus cuneifolius (Sand blackberry)

Rubus aboriginum (Garden dewberry)

Rubus alaskensis (Alaska blackberry)

Rubus chamaemorus (Cloudberries)

Rubus audax (Tampa blackberry)

Rubus deliciosus (Delicious Raspberry)

Rubus felix (Woodland dewberries)

Rubus glaucifolius (San Diego raspberry)

Rubus persistens (Persistent blackberries)

Rubus mirus (Marvel dewberries)

Rubus ulmifolius (Elmleaf dewberries)

Rubus setosus (Setose blackberry)

Sambucus nigra (Blue elderberry)

Sambucus racemosa (Red Elderberry)

Sorbus scopulina (European Mountain Ash)

Vaccinium alaskaense (Alaska blueberry)

Vaccinium angustifolium (Lowbush blueberry)

Vaccinium arboreum (Farkleberry)

Vaccinium boreale (Northern blueberry)

Vaccinium caesariense (New Jersey blueberry)

Vaccinium reticulatum (Ohelo blueberries)

Vaccinium calycinum (Ohelo blueberries) (again)

Vand accinium dentatum (all called Ohelo blueberries)

Vaccinium cespitosum (Dwarf bilberry)

Vaccinium corymbosum (Highbush blueberry)

Vaccinium crassifolium (Creeping blueberry)

Vaccinium darrowii (Darrow's blueberry)

Vaccinium deliciosum (Cascade bilberry)

Vaccinium elliottii (Elliott's blueberry)

Vaccinium erythrocarpum (Southern mountain cranberry)

Vaccinium formosum (Southern blueberry)

Vaccinium fuscatum (black highbush blueberry)

Vaccinium hirsutum (Hairy blueberry)

Vaccinium macrocarpon (Cranberry)

Vaccinium membranaceum (Thinleaf huckleberry)

Vaccinium myrsinites (Shiny blueberry)

Vaccinium myrtilloides (Velvetleaf huckleberry)

Vaccinium myrtillus (Whortleberry)

Vaccinium ovalifolium (Oval-leaf blueberry)

Vaccinium ovatum (California huckleberry)

Vaccinium oxycoccos (Small cranberry)

Vaccinium pallidum (Blue Ridge blueberry)

Vaccinium parvifolium (Red huckleberry)

Vaccinium scoparium (Grouse whortleberry)

Vaccinium simulatum (Upland highbush blueberry)

Vaccinium stamineum (Deerberry)

Vaccinium tenellum (Small black blueberry)

Vaccinium uliginosum (Bog blueberry)

Vaccinium virgatum (Smallflower blueberry)

Vaccinium vitis-idaea (Lingonberry)

Vitis aestivalis (Summer Grape)

Vitis riparia (Riverbank grape)

Vitis acerifolia (Mapleleaf grape)

Vitis arizonica (Canyon grape)

Vitis californica (California wild grape)

Vitis cinerea (Graybark grape)

Vitis girdiana (Wild desert grape)

Vitis labrusca (Fox grape)

Vitis monticola (Sweet mountain grape)

Vitis mustangensis (Mustang grape)

Vitis palmata (Catbird grape)

Vitis rotundifolia (Muscadine grape)

Vitis rupestris (Sand grape)

Vitis vinifera (Wine grape)

Vitis vulpina (Frost grape)

Poisons

Actaea pachypoda (pokeweed): some people say healthy adults may eat up to ten berries. Others say no.

Bromus catharticus: poisonous grass

Bromus purgans: poisonous grass

Bryonia alba (white bryony): berries and all parts poisonous

Chamaesyce, all species (asthma plant): poisonous

Datura inoxia (sacred datura): poisonous

Datura stramonium (jimsonweed): poisonous

Eragrostis megastachya (stinkgrass): poisonous grass

Holcus lanatus (common velvetgrass): poisonous grass

Iris missouriensis (Rocky Mountain iris): poisonous

Lolium temulentum (poison darnel): poisonous grass

Ranunculus acris (buttercup): poisonous

Rhamnus cathartica (common buckthorn): berries are purgative

Senecio jacobaea (tansy ragwort): poisonous, all parts

Senecio vulgaris (common groundsel): poisonous, all parts

Solanum dulcamara (bittersweet nightshade): poisonous

Veratrum californicum (California false-hellebore): poisonous

Zigadenus paniculatus (foothill death camas): poisonous, all parts)

Questions and Answers

Q: I notice that you avoid technical botanical terms when describing plants. For example, what you call "berries," others might technically term "drupes" or "fruits" or other terms. Why?

A: I specifically avoided botanical jargon when writing this book because I wanted the book to be easily useful to everyone, which starts with using common, not technical, terms. If you are looking for technical botanical information on the plants found in this book, you can search the scientific names listed here in the U.S. Department of Agriculture plant database, found online at plants.usda.gov, or at Plants for a Future, found online at pfaf.org.

Q: You say you want this book to focus on usefulness and common language, but you have listed all the plants by their Latin names rather than their common names.

A: When practicing plant identification, it is critical to use Latin names rather than common names because Latin names are the only way to be accurate. For example, there are dozens of plants in the U.S. that are called "pigweed," including several species in this book. There is no safe way to teach people about edible "pigweed" because that word refers to different plants depending on where you live and who taught you the lingo. I grew up in a very small town that used pioneer and regional names for many plants that, I discovered later, were commonly known by different names in more densely populated areas of my state. Today, people use the internet to search for information about edible plants, and if you search by common name instead of scientific name, you get a dangerously unreliable Wild West of information—info that ranges from completely false to dangerously misguided to correct. The most important consideration when scouting for wild edibles is safety, and there is no way to be safe when using common names because they change sometimes from county to county, let alone state by state. I can't tell you how many times I've had people in my classes say, "That's what pigweed looks like? I always thought pigweed looked like something else." And they are right, pigweed means many things to many people and some versions are edible and some are possibly poisonous, so Latin names are crucial for safety. If you are not familiar with using Latin names, take the time to get comfortable with them before attempting to research or scout wild edibles.

Q: You discuss the importance of Latin names, but some plants in this book have one or more Latin synonyms. In addition, some of the online resources and print books don't seem to match the Latin names that you use in this book. Help!

A: You have stumbled upon one of the great frustrations of botany—changing scientific names. I have strong opinions about this: It needs to stop. Once upon a time, scientific names were changed rarely, if there were strong reasons to do so. Today, thousands if not tens of thousands of plants have been renamed, and it seems that each year more names are changed. Why? My explanation is this: University botany professors and doctoral researchers used to discover plants. Today, they seem to focus on renaming them in a fight for relevance. Discovering new plants has become difficult, and many of the new species to be discovered are in places that are either dangerous because of war or hostility to outsiders, or are dangerous because they are in extreme locales. I think it's safe to say the easy botanical discoveries have been made. In addition, there are now far more botany professionals, each of them fighting for funding, resources, and attention in a world where university herbariums are being tossed out instead of expanded. Tenure and teaching positions depend on botanists making a name for themselves and presenting papers at endless conferences. In short, they struggle for relevance and try to make a name for themselves in any way they can, including making arguments to their fellow scholars to convince them to change scientific names that have been long established. The practical impact of all this has been seismic. Books published only a century ago now sometimes spread confusion because some of the scientific names have been changed. Many websites and printed books list different Latin names for the same plants. Anyone who wants to learn about plants finds themselves trapped in an ever-changing miasma of changing names. All of this is compounded by the endless arguments over what are genuine species and what are subspecies. How many species of elderberries are there in nature, really? Decades have been spent arguing, and the arguing will probably only continue, at least until botanists come to their senses and take responsibility for the damage they are doing to the common understanding of plants. Meanwhile, the people who have to deal with such nonsense have sort of given up. The U.S. Department of Agriculture plant database, instead of trying to weigh in on the nonsense, simply lists them all. The same plants are listed multiple times under different species names and different subspecies names. I do not blame the USDA—what other choice so they have? They cannot arbitrate the ridiculousness. The International Association of Botanical and Mycological Societies has not shown the will power to put an end to the damage that unnecessary names changes strews in its wake. They allow this to continue for selfish reasons, and I call on them to stop. Changing names should be rare. Each time a name is changed, it damages the efforts of the rest of us to participate in botany. The mess left behind, both in print and online, will never be cleaned up. Shame on those who vote in favor of these changes. I recognize that these are strong words, but I think they are warranted. No more botanical name changes unless there is a reason compelling enough to warrant the eternal confusion the changes leave behind!

Q: I have tasted a plant that you list in this book and I disagree with the flavor you have listed. For example, I tasted X berry and you said it was sweet and it was tart. I tasted Y green that you said was mild and it was bitter! Why?

A: Peak flavor exists only for a short time. If you harvest a berry even hours before it is fully ripe, it will be tart or bitter instead of sweet. All plants can be bitter if exposed to drought, or if picked after the flower stalk appears, because this changes the plant. Most plants taste best when tender. For greens this means early. For berries this mean when soft. For roots it means at peak storage instead of when the plant is using the energy stored in the root or tuber for growth. You may have to return to a wild plant several times before you find it at peak harvest time.

Q: How did you identify the species by flower color when the color of many flowers is often more than one color?

A: The organization of flowers by color in this book is meant as a general guide. Trying to define the color of a flower can quickly become an exercise in futility and frustration. Flower color refers to the dominant color. This book makes no attempt to wade into the complex and fraught business of identifying technical botanical flower parts, where even experts struggle to agree on some species. Some flower colors vary based on subspecies. Flower color may also vary by sex in a single species, and sometimes, to complicate matters, flowers of a different sex are on the same plant. To complicate matters further, plants have many sexual orientation options beyond male and female. Sometimes it is helpful to remember that classification is simply a human construct attempting to describe what Mother Nature does without human approval, nor any interest in human approval, of her work. Flower refers to the part of the plant that a common person in the field would likely identify as the flower. Many flowers also have minor colors. Some species with purple flowers often also occur as white, depending on genetics and other factors; *Calochortus* species have many examples of this. Other examples include red flowers that come in shades of orange, white flowers that sometimes appear in shades of pale green, and blue flowers come in shades of purple. The same species might

be predominantly white in one area and purple in another. Flower colors on some species can change according to temperature, age, drought, available light, soil nutrients, season, and natural genetic variation. Some flower variations may only appear rarely. Never eat any wild edible unless you know its identification at an expert level. Please also note that flower colors and appearance may become highly changed or deformed if the plant has been exposed to chemicals such as glyphosate or has become glyphosate-tolerant or adapted. Examples of this are often found on roadsides and fieldsides.

Q: Do some wild edibles have dangerous look-alikes?

A: Yes. Never eat any wild edible unless you are sure you know you have correct identification. Always eat wild edibles in small amounts, to be safe. Take a class from a wild edible expert in your area or join a group of like-minded people. Be smart and safe. Questions? Concerns? Find me at SeedRenaissance@gmail.com, SeedRenaissance.com, or facebook.com/caleb.warnock.